52typo

52typo
52 stories on type, typography and graphic design

Concept by
Linda Kudrnovská, Michel Chanaud

Managing Editor
Linda Kudrnovská

Contributing Editors
Jakub Skalický, Silvia Sfligiotti, Dionysis Livanis, Dan Reynolds

Copy Editor
Elizabeth Walsh Spacilova

Design
Filip Blažek, Designiq

Image Editor
David Dubec, Designiq

Printed by
D'Auria Printing, Italy

Paper
Magno Natural 140g

Typefaces
Inka by Carnoky Type & Stratos by Production Type

Unsigned articles are by the editors.
Unless otherwise noted, all photographs and illustrations are from the archive
of the author of the article.
We have taken all reasonable steps to find possible copyright holders.
If you can claim authorship, please notify the publisher and we will publish
a suitable mention in the next edition of *52typo*.

ISBN 978-3-7212-0975-4

© English edition 2017 Niggli, imprint of Braun Publishing AG, Salenstein
www.niggli.ch

The original version was published by étapes: editions, Paris

52typo

52 stories on type, typography and graphic design

niggli

Contents

p. 82

p. 52

p. 58

p. 94

p. 79

p. 164

p. 158

p. 170

p. 186

FAREWELL

01

52 weeks of type, typography and graphic design

TEXT BY LINDA KUDRNOVSKÁ

What is graphic design? Why do we still need new typefaces? How are famous logos created? Where do the boundaries of the designer's responsibility lie when his or her work is used to serve ideology? What does lettering in Amazonia look like? Why didn't New Zealand adopt a new flag? And what did Alan Rickman do before he became an actor?

The answers to these questions and many more can be found in the debut edition of *52typo*. Published in cooperation with Association Typographique Internationale, *52typo* presents 52 unique stories on type, typography and graphic design from cities as diverse as Buenos Aires, Delhi, Istanbul, London, Melbourne, Mexico City, New York, Paris, Prague, Seoul, Tel Aviv and Tehran.

The book will acquaint readers with the past year's most important news in the field of graphic design and typography – from original projects, major milestones and inspiring events to interesting publications and essays contributed by forty renowned authors and designers from all over the world.

The stories in this book are a selection of the very best from *365typo: Stories on type, typography and graphic design*, vol. 2. Whereas the scope of *365typo* makes it primarily intended for professionals, the book you are holding in your hands also contains previously unpublished images, new stories and information that no longer made it into the larger publication.

52typo. A new inspiring story for every week.

02
New Perspectives in Typography

TEXT BY FILIP BLAŽEK

New Perspectives in Typography is sort of an exhibition catalogue, but for an exhibition that never happened.

In it, author-curators Scott Williams and Henrik Kubel have chosen works by over 100 designers from twenty countries whom they believe, as they explain in the introduction, represent "an intelligent, thoughtful and, above all, inspirational use of typography".

The authors have an exceptionally broad-ranging perspective and do not limit themselves to any particular style or genre, and this remarkable view of how typefaces are used today increases the value of the entire publication. Readers can find samples of very serious type designs in newspapers, corporate identities and navigation systems, but also dozens of impressive posters and book and magazine covers that prove there still are plenty of new ideas and original uses for type. Nor do the authors avoid other aspects of typography. The book looks not only at type design, but also at how the field has opened up to the greater public, whether through the film *Helvetica* or retail type design mugs, T-shirts and notebooks in brick-and-mortar stores.

But the book is far more than a mere showcase of early 21st-century graphic design; the authors also provide pointed insight on the works they chose, placing them in a broader context. This, too, evokes the idea of an exhibition, where the important exhibits feature a headphone icon. As a bonus, the book features brilliant essays by Paul Shaw, Monika Parrinder & Colin Davies, Emily King and Rick Poynor, who speak about historical influences on contemporary typography and the relationship between art and type, or search for the answer to the question of where the democratization of type design will lead us in the coming years.

Scott Williams & Henrik Kubel:
New Perspectives in Typography
Laurence King, London, United Kingdom,
September 2015
Softcover, 304 pp., 245 × 190 mm

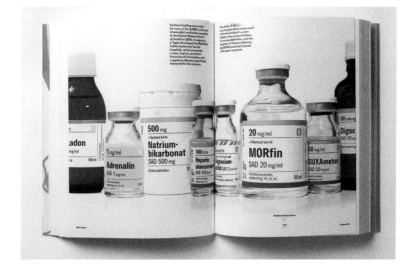

CATO
COZZOLINO
EMERY
FLETT
KIDD
KIN-YEE
LANCASHIRE
NOWLAND
SADGROVE
SPATCHURST
TUCKER
TURNER
WILLIAMSON

03

On the Shoulders of Giants

TEXT BY STEPHEN BANHAM

Thirteen Australian graphic designers in a single documentary and book.

Back in 2008, Australia's most venerable graphic designers were individually interviewed in a hotel over a single weekend. The result is the ambitious *On the Shoulders of Giants*, a documentary and book of these varied figures whose design practices were prominent in the mid to late 20th century.

Taking a couple of years to finally come to fruition, the project was produced and funded by various members of the design community.

The interviews are now housed within a casebound book along with further texts offering deeper insights into the evolution of their practices. These include such design luminaries as Les Mason, Ken Cato, Garry Emery and Mimmo Cozzolino, amongst many others.

The authors of the project say, "The documentary is not so much about their work. It's about who they are as people and what makes them do what they do. Their talent, energy, sense of humour and ability to transform ideas into the signs of our times have played, and continue to play, a significant role in influencing Australian life. Building on the earlier foundations of a very few, these people have not only helped change how we see ourselves and how others see us, they have also helped shape the visual communications industry in Australia today."

In keeping with the Australian flavour, the display face used throughout both the film titling and print material is Albion Sans, designed by the Melbourne-based type studio Letterbox, who were also the designers of the book.

This project has already become an important resource for future students and scholars of Australian graphic design culture and a tribute to those who have helped shape the graphic design industry in Australia today.

Larissa Meikle, Kate McDonald:
On the Shoulders of Giants
Graffiti Design, Australia, 2014
(released in 2015)
Hardcover, 72 pp., 145 × 265 mm

04

Atelier National de Recherche Typographique, the book 1985–2006

TEXT BY ISABELLE MOISY

To echo the exhibit hosted at the Ministry of Cultural Affairs, the director of the Atelier National de Recherche Typographique (ANRT), typographer Thomas Huot-Marchand, revisits the editorial and graphic concepts behind the catalogue, which was designed by Olivier Huz and Ariane Bosshard.

ANRT was established in 1985 to reinvigorate what was a struggling field back then: typeface design. Its mission was soon widened to include typographical research and practice. Initially located at the Imprimerie Nationale, then at Paris's ENSAD and finally at Nancy's École nationale supérieure d'art et de design, it educated over one hundred student-researchers between 1985 and 2006 and contributed to the French scene's spectacular resurgence. After a six-year hiatus, the Atelier reopened in Nancy with a new team and research project.

ISABELLE MOISY: **In what context was this catalogue produced? What was the editorial project?**
THOMAS HUOT-MARCHAND: Editing this catalogue became an obvious necessity as soon as I took over as the director of ANRT in the autumn of 2012. I was preparing the re-opening of the Atelier after it had been closed for six years: nothing had ever been published in the first twenty years, and I subsequently initiated a program to valorize the archives, which meant digitizing the entire stock kept in Nancy.

How was the book put together? How did you imagine its structure, especially in relation to the region's history?
As we were thinking this publication through, three main parts took shape. The beginning, a history of the ANRT, was handed over to Sébastien Morlighem (for the 1979–1991 period) and Roxane Jubert (1991–2006). Following this comes a selection of the best research projects carried out at the ANRT, organized as eight thematic chapters. The third part is a biographical index of all of the Atelier's former teachers and students.

Why choose Olivier and Ariane for this editorial object? What is their relationship to the ANRT? To its former students, collaborators or regular speakers?
I immediately thought of them because I greatly admire their work and the intelligence of their editorial produc-

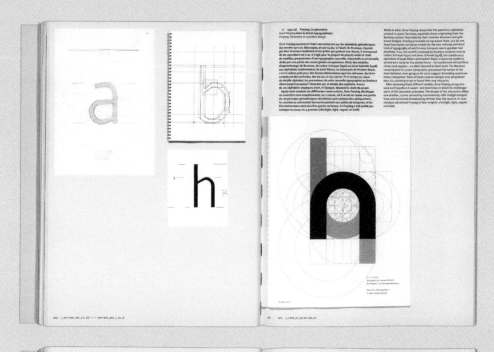

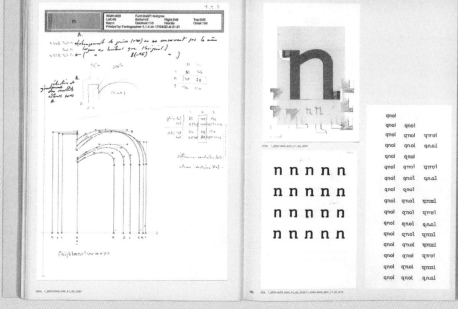

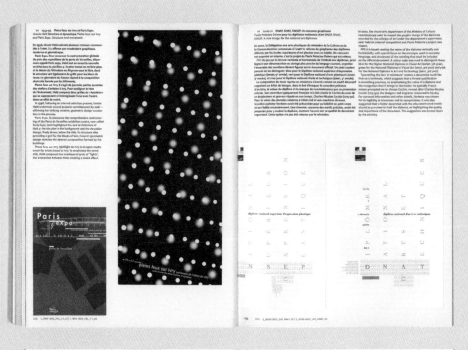

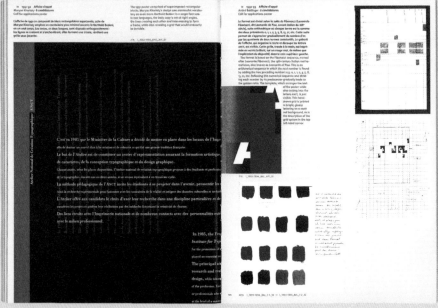

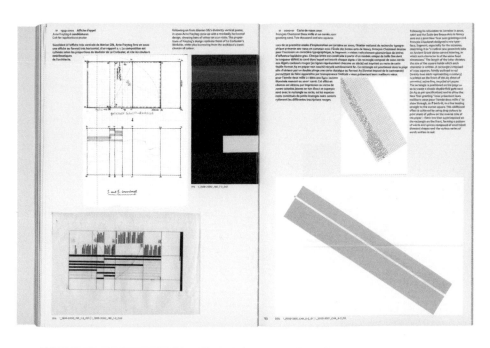

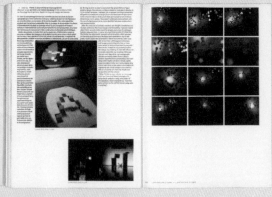

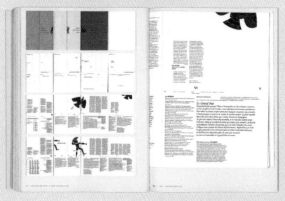

tion. I really wanted to entrust this mission to graphic designers who weren't from the ANRT and would have a fresh perspective on it. They are also good friends, which allowed us to face this huge undertaking with trust and good spirits.

How did former students and teachers collaborate with the ANRT?
It's one of the great successes of this project: I was able to contact nearly all the alumni (which was no easy task, even though only a few years have passed) to go back to various projects and find documents that were missing from our shelves. Former teachers such as Rudi Meyer, Hans-Jürg Hunziker, Albert Boton and Jean Widmer also took part in the project. In fact, there were emotional reunions at the catalogue launch in Paris. Finally, I am very happy that François Barré and Christian Debize could write the foreword, because they are two characters who played a great role in the Atelier's history.

What is it that makes this book unique?
Its content is unique because it has largely remained unpublished till now. The iconographic material inside is very rare: one can follow every step in the creation of a new font, from the first sketches to stabilizing the design. The 1985–2006 period covers two decades during which this profession went from essentially analogue methods to largely digital work. To measure these changes, special attention was brought to the nature of the documents we reproduced (exclusively work-in-progress documents, at various stages) and the quality of their reproductions.

The production of this catalogue was made possible by extensive collaboration among companies involved in Lorraine's book industry, as they took care of digitizing the content (Stacomest, Essey-lès-Nancy), printing (Shareprint, Maxéville) and binding (Clément, Nancy-Seichamps) the catalogue, and manufacturing the paper (Clairefontaine, Étival-Clairefontaine). Publication of the catalogue was supported by the region's prefecture as part of the EU's European Regional Development Fund 2007–2013, the Ministry of Cultural Affairs and Communication, and Imprimerie nationale.

Originally published in *étapes: 231* (May–June 2016).

Thomas Huot-Marchand, Roxane Jubert and Sébastien Morlighem:
ANART Archives 1985–2006
Éditions Les Presses du réel, Dijon / ANRT, Nancy, France, 2016
Hardcover, 322 pp., 238 × 325 mm

05
Beyond my control

TEXT BY MARTIN MAJOOR

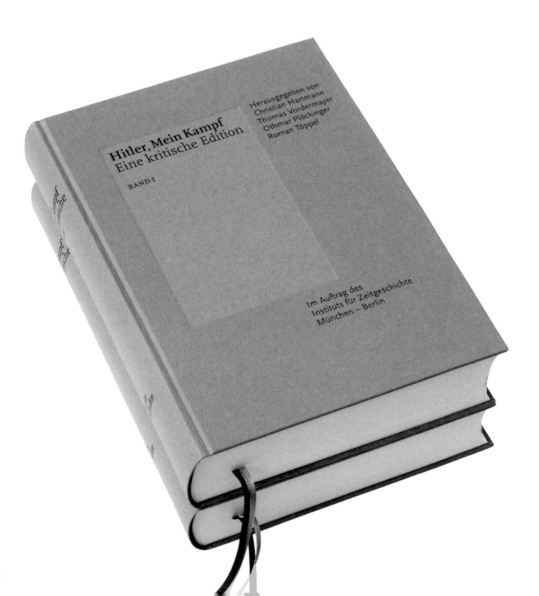

Hitler, Mein Kampf:
Eine kritische Edition
Commissioned by the
Institute of Contem-
porary History (IfZ),
Munich / Berlin, 2016
Hardcover, 2 volumes,
210 × 280 mm

Long ago I had a discussion with a book typographer about the importance of type design versus book design. When he was designing a book, he told me, he felt like an architect designing a building. The title page was the monumental entrance, the chapters were the rooms, the type area was like a window and the cover was the eye-catching roof over the building.

It was a nice comparison that even went on when he started comparing the micro typography with the details in the building. But the discussion became acrimonious when he turned to me and stated that the type designer was merely baking the bricks for the building, while the printer was the bricklayer and the bookbinder was the roofer.

Of course I did not agree, not only as a type designer, but in general. I could have replied something like, "You may feel like the architect but most of your books look like terraced houses and the quality of my bricks make these houses at least have some grandeur." But I didn't reply in this childish way simply because I felt that a book is a complex product, a collaboration between author, publisher, book designer, papermaker, type designer, printer, bookbinder and bookseller. Except for the author, all people involved have a servant role.

The role of the book designer is considerable, especially when it comes to the choice of the typeface. As a living type designer it is quite satisfying when my typeface is being chosen, whether it's for a book, a poster, a website or a sign system. Often when I am confronted with my typeface in use, it makes me feel proud. But not always.

My type, but not my type of values
Sometimes my types are used by organizations that don't meet with my approval. I had mixed feelings when a far-right political party started using one of my typefaces, especially when they did it in a really good way. It felt as if I willy-nilly contributed to the popularization of right-wing values. Should I be happy for the good use of my typeface, or should I be sad for the fact that it was being used by

1. Band / 5. Kapitel / Der Weltkrieg

39 Diesen Satz hat Hitler wiederholt muß ert. Er wurde später von seinen Gegnern oft aufgegriffen, da er Fragen nach seinem Militärdienst aufwarf. Ob Hitler nach München umzog, um der Stellungspflicht in Österreich zu entgehen, ist nach wie vor umstritten. Belegt ist, dass er sich am 5. 2. 1914 in Salzburg einer Nachmusterung unterziehen musste und dabei für »waffenuntauglich« befunden wurde. Als sicher gelten darf zudem, dass der Zeitpunkt von Hitlers Umzug im Mai 1913 keineswegs nur »politische«, sondern erste Linie ökonomische Gründe hatte: Sein väterliches Erbe konnte erst an seinem 24. Geburtstag (20. 4. 1913) ausgezahlt werden.
Vgl. Plöckinger, Texte, S. 96–100; Plöckinger, Geschichte, S. 72, 77, 179 f., 208; Kap. 1/4, Anm. 1.

40 Ludwig III. von Bayern (1845–1921), 1912/13 Prinzregent für seinen geisteskranken Cousin König Otto I., 1913–1918 letzter König von Bayern.

41 Hitlers Darstellung ist aus mehreren Gründen unglaubwürdig: Erstens war nicht die Kabinettskanzlei ermächtigt, Ausländer als Freiwillige anzunehmen, sondern allein das Kriegsministerium; Hitler war zu dieser Zeit noch österreichischer Staatsbürger. Zweitens ist es äußerst unwahrscheinlich, dass die Beamten in der Situation des Kriegsausbruchs Hitlers Gesuch innerhalb eines Tages bearbeiteten, beantworteten und ihm zustellten. Drittens haben sich keine Belege für dieses Immediatgesuch erhalten, obwohl das Bayerische Kriegsarchiv schon 1924 danach geforscht hat. Und viertens kam Hitler erst am 16. 8. 1914 zum Ersatz-Bataillon des 2. Infanterie-Regiments, also knapp zwei Wochen nach der angeblichen Genehmigung seines Immediatgesuchs. Sehr wahrscheinlich meldete sich Hitler Anfang August 1914 einfach beim nächstliegenden Truppenteil und wurde angenommen. Ob dabei seine österreichische Staatsbürgerschaft übersehen wurde, ist unklar; möglicherweise profitierte Hitler auch entscheidend von dem »juristischen Rat«, den ihm der Assessor Ernst Hepp in dieser Sache erteilt hatte. Am 1. 9. 1914 wurde er schließlich der 1. Kompanie des Reserve-Infanterie-Regiments Nr. 16 zugewiesen.
Vgl. BayHStA, Kriegsarchiv, Bay. Reserve-Infanterie-Regiment Nr. 16, 3046. R/StR, Bd. 2, Eintrag 1062; Joachimsthaler, Weg, S. 100–108; Kershaw, Hitler, Bd. 1, S. 128 f.; Weber, Krieg, S. 15 f.; Plöckinger, Soldaten, S. 28; Pyta, Hitler, Zitat S. 122.

daß mein Platz dann dort sein mußte, wo mich die innere Stimme nun einmal hinwies.

Aus politischen Gründen hatte ich Österreich in erster Linie verlassen³⁹; was war aber nun² selbstverständlicher, als daß ich nun, da der Kampf begann, dieser Gesinnung erst recht Rechnung tragen mußte.² Ich wollte nicht für die Habsburgischen Staat fechten, war aber bereit, für mein Volk und das dieses verkörpernde Reich jederzeit zu sterben.

Am 3. August reichte ich ein Immediatgesuch an Seine Majestät König Ludwig III.⁴⁰ ein mit der Bitte, in ein bayerisches Regiment eintreten zu dürfen. Die Kabinettskanzlei hatte in diesen Tagen sicherlich nicht wenig zu tun; um so größer war meine Freude, als ich schon am Tage darauf die Erledigung meiner Ansuchens erhielt. Als ich mit zitternden Händen das Schreiben geöffnet hatte und die Genehmigung meiner Bitte mit der Aufforderung las, mich bei einem bayerischen Regiment zu melden, kannte² Jubel und Dankbarkeit keine Grenze². Wenige Tage später zog ich dann den Rock, den ich erst nach nahezu sechs Jahren wieder ausziehen sollte.⁴¹

So, wie wohl für jeden Deutschen, begann nun auch für mich die unvergeßlichste und größte Zeit meines irdischen Lebens.⁴² Gegenüber den Ereignissen dieses gewaltigsten Ringens fiel alles Vergangene in ein schales Nichts zurück. Mit stolzer Wehmut denke ich gerade in diesen Tagen, da sich zum zehnten Male das gewaltige Geschehen jährt, zurück an diese Wochen des beginnenden Heldenkampfes unseres Volkes, den mitzumachen mir das Schicksal gnädig erlaubte.⁴³

Wie gestern erst zieht an mir Bild um Bild vorbei, sehe ich mich im Kreise meiner lieben Kameraden eingekleidet, dann zum ersten Male ausrücken, exerzieren usw., bis endlich der Tag des Ausmarsches kam.

Eine einzige Sorge quälte mich in dieser Zeit, mich wie so viele andere auch, ob wir nicht zu spät zur Front kommen würden. Das allein ließ mich oft und oft nicht Ruhe finden. So blieb in jedem Siegesjubel über eine neue Heldentat im ganzen Zimmer her um, fortgerissen von seiner Phantasie.» Am 29. 6. 1924 berichtete Heß seiner Verlobten, Hitler habe ihm die Schilderung seiner »Feuertaufe« vorgelesen und sei dabei zu Tränen gerührt gewesen.

1926: gestrichen: nun

1939: Punkt ersetzt durch: Ausrufezeichen

1944: kannte ersetzt durch: kannten
1944: Grenze ersetzt durch: Grenzen

1930: unsere Verzögerung ersetzt durch: unseres Zuspätkommens

42 In der Weimarer Republik prägte die Glorifizierung des Kriegserlebnisses die Erinnerung an den Ersten Weltkrieg. In Rechtfertigungsschriften hoher Militärs, aber auch in amtlichen Publikationen wie *Der Weltkrieg 1914–1918* dominierte zunächst der »Blick von oben«. Daneben aber entwickelte sich eine andere literarische Erinnerung an den Weltkrieg, die auch Vertreter des »soldatischen Nationalismus« wie Franz Schauwecker oder Ernst Jünger einschloss. Mit ihren nationalistischen »Reportagen« vom Schlachtfeld waren sie eine Herausforderung für die amtliche Militärgeschichtsschreibung des 1919 gegründeten Reichsarchivs, das

zunächst ganz in der Tradition der Operationsgeschichtsschreibung des Großen Generalstabs stand. Am 3. 5. 1924 konstatierte die Nachrichtenstelle im Reichswehrministerium in einem Schreiben an das Reichsarchiv, dass sich das »Erstarken der nationalen Idee und die Sehnsucht nach Wiederbelebung der Wehrfähigkeit unseres Volkes« unter anderem an »dem zur Zeit bestehenden Verlangen nach Veröffentlichung von Kriegserinnerungen« zeige; diesem müsse das Reichsarchiv nun verstärkt Rechnung tragen. Um die nationalistisch-heroisierende Deutungshoheit über das »Fronterlebnis« nicht zu gefährden, begann das

Reichsarchiv, seine Schriftenreihen zu diversifizieren; sie trugen entweder amtlichen Charakter wie *Der Weltkrieg 1914–1918*, sollten das populäre Interesse am Krieg bedienen, etwa in Form der *Schlachten des Weltkrieges*, oder unterstützten die Veteranenpublizistik, die mehrere Hundert *Erinnerungsblätter* umfasste.
Vgl. Müller, Kriegsgeschichte, S. 43, 45; Müller, Krieg, S. 21–35; Ulrich, Perspektive, S. 52 ff.; Hettling/Jeismann, Weltkrieg, S. 209–212; Ulrich/Ziemann (Hrsg.), Krieg, S. 69 f., 77; Zitat S. 69; Pöhlmann, Kriegsgeschichte, S. 79 ff.

43 Über die Entstehung der folgenden Passagen zu Hitlers Kriegserlebnissen schrieb Rudolf Heß am 16. 1. 1924 an seine Mutter: »Eben höre ich aus dem gemeinsamen Wohn- und EßZimmer seine [Hitlers] Stimme. Er scheint mitten im Auffrischen von Kriegserlebnissen zu sein, er ahmt Granaten und Maschinengewehre nach, springt wild im ganzen Zimmer her um, fortgerissen von seiner Phantasie.» Am 29. 6. 1924 berichtete Heß seiner Verlobten, Hitler habe ihm die Schilderung seiner »Feuertaufe« vorgelesen und sei dabei zu Tränen gerührt gewesen.
Vgl. Heß, Briefe, Zitate S. 324, 341 f.

44 Die Eroberung von Lüttich (16. 8. 1914) und Brüssel (20. 8. 1914) sowie die erfolgreiche Schlacht in Lothringen (20.–22. 8. 1914) schienen in Deutschland die Hoffnung auf einen raschen Sieg zu bestätigen. Angesichts der Erfolge der 6. Armee unter Führung des bayerischen Kronprinzen Rupprecht bei Metz am 20. 8. 1914 herrschte vor allem in München große Euphorie.
Vgl. Münchner Neueste Nachrichten vom 23. 8. 1914, »Der Sieg in Lothringen«; Frankfurter Zeitung vom 20. 8. 1914 (2. MA), »Gute Zuversicht«.

458

459

---

such an organization? It is clear that the choice of type is beyond my control.

In 2016 an infamous book was published in Germany: Hitler's *Mein Kampf* ("My Struggle"). The choice of type was Scala and Scala Sans, a type family I had designed at the end of the 1980s. When I learned about its use in the book, I didn't know what to think of it.

An ethical approach

This new edition of *Mein Kampf* is definitely not a simple reprint of Hitler's bestseller from 1925 (with over one million copies sold in many countries). It is an annotated, critical version with a huge amount of commentaries encircling Hitler's original text. It has been conceived as a scientific document and it is meant to be used by scholars, not by the neo-Nazi movement.

Rudolf Paulus Gorbach, the book designer responsible for the typography, wanted to create a clear visual structure without any fashionable clichés. One of the ways to achieve this was by choosing a good typeface. He tried out several typefaces, one of them being Trump Mediaeval, his personal favorite. But when he found out Georg Trump, the type designer, had volunteered in Hitler's army, it was clear to him this typeface could not be used for this purpose. He

argued that the elements, of which the book was made up, like the paper and typeface, could not have any connection to people possibly working during the Nazi era.

Scala was a suitable typeface not only because it has a serif and a sans version, but also because it was designed in 1989 by an independent type designer born in 1960 in the Netherlands – in other words, in no way connected to the Nazi era. As always, the choice of the typeface was beyond my control, but this time I didn't feel my typeface was "contributing" to the popularization of this anti-Semitic manifesto. I couldn't suppress a certain feeling of pride for the fact that my typeface was part of this typographic masterpiece. Am I allowed to feel this way in such a case?

In a complex, collaborative product like a book, the type designer is almost never involved as a person. When I am dead, my typefaces will live on and I certainly have no influence on the choice of type. But since I'm alive I have learned to accept that the choice of my typeface is beyond my control.

Seeing your own typeface in use can make you feel proud. But what if it is used to design something that goes against your fundamental principles and convictions?

Martin Majoor

ALPHABETA
CLASSIC

———

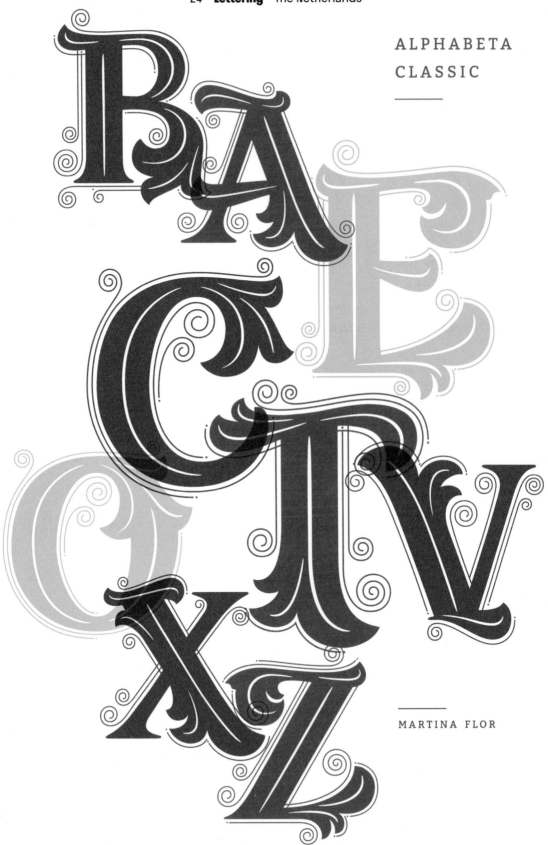

———

MARTINA FLOR

06

Dutch Alphabets:
A new Dutch lettering model book

TEXT BY MATHIEU LOMMEN

Lettering model books provide professionals with models for imitation, such as alphabets and fictional uses. The Netherlands has a rich tradition of producing printed manuals for the teaching of writing and lettering.

The engraved writing books of the Dutch Golden Age, especially those made by the illustrious master Jan van den Velde, were influential throughout Europe in the 17th and 18th centuries.

In the 1830s printed lettering model books began to be published in great numbers internationally as well. The invention of lithography made it technically easier to produce illustrated editions and also carved out its own niche, as lithographers were expected to transfer not only images but also text to stone. These manuals – in book form or as portfolios – were also in demand among anyone else professionally involved in lettering. Often the illustrations were beautifully printed in solid colours.

Having researched this area for some years now at the University of Amsterdam, I was taken by the idea of producing such a luxurious loose-leaf album myself, printed in PMS solid colours and featuring samples by some of today's most prominent "Dutch" lettering artists, type designers, lettercutters, calligraphers and sign painters. "Dutch" in this context means that the contributor had to be born and/or received a graphic design education in the Netherlands. With this idea in mind and a provisional list in hand, my collaboration with Peter Verheul began. Everyone we approached enthusiastically agreed to collaborate on the project pro bono. The generosity of all concerned certainly helped us find a publisher quickly.

The limited-edition *Dutch Alphabets* contains 46 broadsides with mostly newly drawn or written alphabets or partial alphabets. Naturally the volume includes quite a few specimens by (former) teachers and students of the Type & Media masters course at the Royal Academy of Art in The Hague. We were also fortunate in securing the cooperation of Gerrit Noordzij and Gerard Unger, the grand old men of Dutch type design. Both left an indelible stamp on the profession.

ABCDEFG
HIJKLMNO
PQRSTUVW
XYZ

Gerard Unger

2

· TICKETS AND INQUIRIES ·
ABCDEFGHIJKLM
· GOLDEN ARROW · EVENING STAR ·
NOPQRSTUVWXYZ
· PLATFORM 3, 4 AND 5 · Erik van Blokland

3

With contributions by Amsterdam Signpainters, Yomar Augusto, Jacques le Bailly (8), Donald Beekman, Françoise Berserik, Barbara Bigosińska, Frank E. Blokland, Erik van Blokland (3), Maria Doreuli (4), James Edmondson, Ramiro Espinoza, Martina Flor (1), Dave Foster, Fritz Grögel, Janno Hahn, Hansje van Halem, Berton Hasebe, Henry van der Horst, Ondrej Jób, Max Kisman, René Knip (7), Holger Königsdörfer, Paul van der Laan, Lida Lopes Cardozo, Niels Shoe Meulman, Ross Milne, Gerrit Noordzij, Diana Ovezea, Krista Radoeva, Trine Rask, Arthur Reinders Folmer, Donald Roos (5), Pieter van Rosmalen, Just van Rossum, Kristyan Sarkis, Florian Schick, Elmo van Slingerland, Heidi Sørensen, Nina Stössinger, Joost Swarte, Teo Tuominen, Underware (9), Gerard Unger (2), Peter Verheul, Bernd Volmer (6) and Job Wouters.

ABCDEFGHIJ
KLMNOPQR
STUVWXYZ

MARIA DOREULI, 2015

4

5

DOUBLE QUAYER POUNDER SERIF BY DONALD ROOS

BERND VOLMER

6

7

ATELIER RENE KNIP | SKETCH FOR AN ARCHITECTURAL ALFABET FOR NIEUWSPOORT THE HAGUE | 2013

8

9

Mathieu Lommen:
Dutch Alphabets:
New Examples of Writing & Lettering
Compiled by Mathieu Lommen & Peter Verheul
De Buitenkant, Amsterdam,
The Netherlands, 2016
Edition of 225 copies, 4 pp., 46 plates,
335 × 240 mm

Type 9010
Czech Digitized Typefaces
1990–2010
www.typo9010.cz

This publication charts
20 years of typeface design
in the Czech Republic, creating
a chronological archive of fonts
and type designers. The book unites
an encyclopaedic collection of
digitized typefaces into one large
"font zoo", with fauna ranging
from the practically lost to the
immensely popular. The fonts are
tested right in texts that describe
the wild Nineties, well-detailed
Noughties and skyrocketing Teens.
This episode in Czech type design
represented a critical period
in its rich history.

BiggBoss © 2015

Tomáš Brousil, Petra Dočekalová (eds.): *Typo 9010*
BiggBoss, Prague, December 2015
Softcover, 288 pp., 220 × 300 mm

07
Typo 9010:
Vive la Compilation

TEXT BY MARTIN PECINA

The team behind
Typo 9010 book: Petra
Dočekalová, editor,
Radek Sidun & Zuzana
Lednická, designers,
Tomáš Brousil, author
of the concept

When I first heard that someone was planning on printing a catalogue of all the typefaces created in what is now the Czech Republic between 1990 and 2010, I made a gesture suggesting someone had a screw loose, turned up my nose and chortled derisively. Indeed, I am no great friend of "collections".

I believe that only in exceptional cases can a meaningful result arise from such a statistical approach to design. Why waste paper on things that may not have any apparent value; for that matter, why let weeds contaminate valuable typefaces? But fortunately, *Typo 9010*, which made such a general, sweeping collection of Czech type its one and only theme, wonderfully proved me guilty of narrow-mindedness and an acutely small imagination.

The set of 399 typefaces by 103 designers covers all of the trends that appeared in the field in minute detail, revealing much about people's thinking and the gradual globalization of the world of type design. It shows the initial enthusiasm following the Velvet Revolution of November 1989, which opened the path to both democracy and the first computers. The early 90s were dominated by type design students studying under Jan Solpera at Prague's Academy of Arts, Architecture and Design (UMPRUM) and their

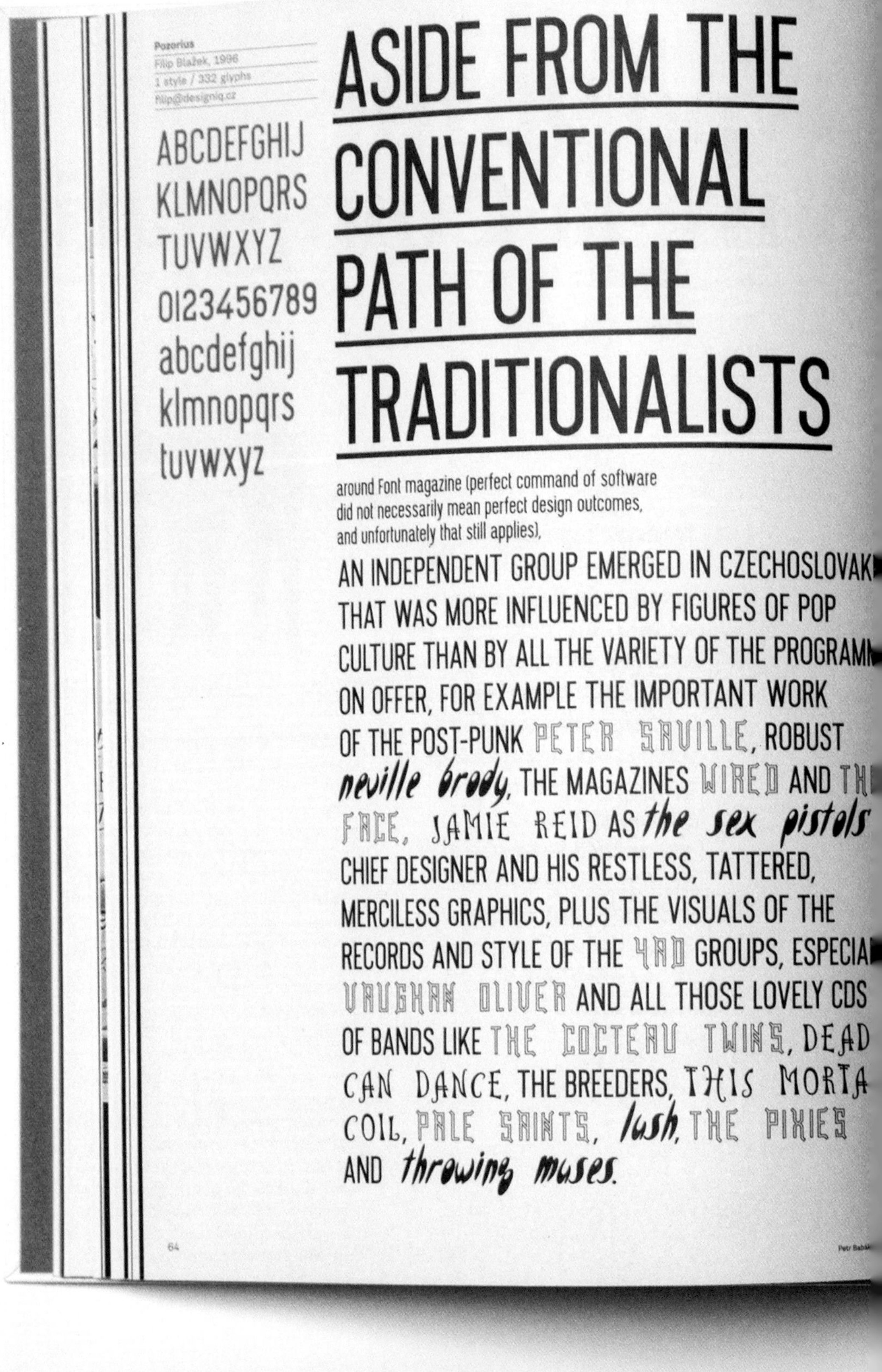

Pozorius
Filip Blažek, 1996
1 style / 332 glyphs
filip@designiq.cz

ABCDEFGHIJ
KLMNOPQRS
TUVWXYZ
0123456789
abcdefghij
klmnopqrs
tuvwxyz

ASIDE FROM THE CONVENTIONAL PATH OF THE TRADITIONALISTS

around Font magazine (perfect command of software
did not necessarily mean perfect design outcomes,
and unfortunately that still applies),

AN INDEPENDENT GROUP EMERGED IN CZECHOSLOVAK
THAT WAS MORE INFLUENCED BY FIGURES OF POP
CULTURE THAN BY ALL THE VARIETY OF THE PROGRAM
ON OFFER, FOR EXAMPLE THE IMPORTANT WORK
OF THE POST-PUNK PETER SAVILLE, ROBUST
neville brody, THE MAGAZINES WIRED AND TH
FACE, JAMIE REID AS the sex pistols
CHIEF DESIGNER AND HIS RESTLESS, TATTERED,
MERCILESS GRAPHICS, PLUS THE VISUALS OF THE
RECORDS AND STYLE OF THE 4AD GROUPS, ESPECIA
VAUGHAN OLIVER AND ALL THOSE LOVELY CDS
OF BANDS LIKE THE COCTEAU TWINS, DEAD
CAN DANCE, THE BREEDERS, THIS MORTA
COIL, PALE SAINTS, lush, THE PIXIES
AND throwing muses.

Petr Babák

Mandragora
Lenka Blažejová, 1996
1 style / 166 glyphs
lnkblajv@gmail.com

Poisson
Radana Lencová, 1996
1 style / 92 glyphs
radana@lencova.eu

ABCDEFGHIJ
KLMNOPQRS
TUVWXYZ
0123456789
abcdefghij
klmnopqrs
tuvwxyz

ABCDEFGHIJ
KLMNOPQRS
TUVWXYZ
0123456789
abcdefghij
klmnopqrs
tuvwxyz

Stroj
David Balihar, 1998
1 style / 66 glyphs
david@02.cz

Timo
Jana Vahalíková, 1996/1997
1 style / 43 glyphs
jana@marvil.cz

0123456789
abcdefghij
klmnopqrs
tuvwxyz

experiments; coincidentally, these very students led Czech graphic design for the following two decades. All of their typefaces share a desire to find a specific expression all of their own, gradually giving way to (a sometimes rather cold) universality.

Contemporary Czech design can no longer be characterized as "local". It is an active proponent of the international typography scene, marked by identical sources of inspiration, solutions and sometimes even similar results. The professionalization of the field, set in the framework of the information society, logically leads to a universal language. The brilliant typefaces by Tomáš Brousil at Suitcase have long been an international phenomenon, as have the ambitious multiscript fonts by Veronika Burian at TypeTogether (see her text on p. 36) and the design team around David Březina's type foundry Rosetta. Perhaps only Radim Peško pursues different goals more clearly in his bespoke typefaces; he uses fashionable trends and postmodern play with anti-traditionalist approaches to achieve a temporary, but to a certain extent unique expression.

The book is accompanied by a knowledgeable chronological record of local events written by designer Filip Blažek, providing the necessary historical context amidst the deluge of typefaces, connecting individual typefaces with a string of important milestones. But the greatest service to the book is Zuzana Lednická's flawless graphic layout, which defies the conventions of typeface specimens. It respectfully highlights exceptional typefaces at the expense of less important ones, adding dynamics to the pages of the book through sudden changes in scale and different ways in which accompanying historical material is inserted. The typefaces are not presented in dummy text; instead, the specimen is set using the articles contributed by one Dutch and several Czech type designers. It is a specimen and the story of Czech type design rolled into one.

Not always does a collection lead to a stinking heap. *Typo 9010* represents an important historical record of everything that has been created in the Czech Republic in its first twenty digital years without forcing a single possible assessment down readers' throats. It will be exciting to see how the next generations, unblemished by communism, revolutionary fervour or the technical difficulties involved in creating a good typeface, follow up on the legacy of these pioneers.

08
Why do we need more typefaces?

TEXT BY VERONIKA BURIAN

As a type designer, every so often one is confronted with the question: "Do we need more typefaces?" As somebody who makes a living out of creating typefaces, the obvious answer is yes; however, there are other less subjective reasons in favour of new type designs.

An effective way of weakening this question usually asked by lay persons is to pose another question, such as "Do we have enough music, or clothes, or art?" In the same spirit, I agree with Cyrus Highsmith's reply "You know, I heard the same thing about people!"

Type design is a carrier of our culture and is subject to developments and trends, even more so in this world of constant movement and change. Type matters more than ever, with increasing self-expression and communication channels, different media and mobile devices that rely heavily on typography for information and coherence of visual identity. Digital fonts and the desktop publishing era have irreversibly changed the process of designing typefaces. The internet and the growing necessity of multilingual, and often multi-script, information pieces have significantly increased the complexity of the type design profession. At the same time, design tools have become faster and easier to use, allowing for a massive flood of digital typefaces on the market. A significant amount of them are novel, short-lived bursts of creativity though often technically and aesthetically flawed. I see no harm in them. They don't waste resources or energy other than the author's own and they are part of our digital online culture, manifested in free, open-source tools and the accompanying enthusiasm of users and creators alike. There is a large gap between the occasional amateur who would create a typeface with limited knowledge and the professional type designer who is providing a very specialized service. These are two extremes that should be differentiated. Font piracy is an obvious issue here, but that goes beyond this essay.

Breaking new ground

Typography is ubiquitous and often taken for granted. Most people don't think about it, as it is just there in their everyday lives to fulfil the many roles type can have. I believe that this existence in the "background" is one of the reasons why the "Do we need more typefaces?" question comes up so often, although it is undoubtedly a valid question from the reader's point of view. The biggest factor in graphic design is communication, and typography is the main contributor. So when graphic designers begin to wonder about the importance of typography, then they really question the essence of their profession and therefore might want to think again. One has to be prepared to move out of an established comfort zone with prescribed recipes and instead

THE ... Swedish Letraset CATALOGUE

the only place that sold it was a special shop on mikulandská street in prague 1

I got "my" letraset catalogue from an experienced graphic designer who had just received a brand new one, so he let me have his old, cut up and worn one. I've had it to this day. It came from sweden. It experienced its golden age while i was a student at the academy of art, architecture and design [aaad] in prague. this was shortly after the 1989 revolution and public photocopy centres started to open up in prague. the best one was on jilská street, their black was completely black, and it was the go-to place for design students and professional graphic designers alike. it was almost like a café/social club; you always knew you'd see a familiar face there. if you were feeling down, you could loiter by the entrance and someone would surely turn up. there were also other options at aaad, such as the phototypesetting machine that worked as a photo enlarger with ready letter templates. the head of the school's printing department.

IN PREVIOUS YEARS, WHEN I TAUGHT A TYPOGRAPHY CLASS AS AN ELECTIVE COURSE, I HAD LEARNED THAT NOT ONLY GRAPHIC DESIGN STUDENTS, BUT ALSO SCULPTORS, GLASSMAKERS AND PAINTERS COULD CREATE INTERESTING CUSTOM TYPES.

I just wasn't sure which year I should assign the work to.

type designers no longer have to depend on whether a type foundry is interested in their work. in fact, the only thing that has remained the same at type foundries is the name; all of their work has been moved to computers that have been fed the right software.

It was a logical development, then, that Andrej Krátky, František Štorm and other students became interested in using computers to execute their designs.

BACK

in the days when students did not regularly carry around their own laptops, I was able to get a Mac for the studio, and later several more.

Meanwhile things have changed. The Iron Curtain disappeared over 20 years ago and the end of the isolation caused the Czechs to start to become more like the rest of Europe. It's logical, of course; one doesn't have to search far for good explanations. Finally Czechs could freely travel, explore the West, absorb capitalist influences and smell more money. Despite the many positive changes, there have also been negative aspects to this development. Nowadays there is no difference between a young type designer growing up in the Czech Republic or Brazil.

THEY ALL GO to study post-graduate courses either in Reading or The Hague. They have the same teachers, watch the same *movies*, read the same *books*, wear the same *clothes* and have the same *opinions*.

Drawing the most beautiful typeface without having vast reading experience should be viewed as an exercise in futility, a misunderstanding of the very sense of the work.

explore new ideas and concepts. Using new typefaces is part of this.

Nevertheless, a type designer should, at least to some extent, think about the driving forces behind creating new fonts. Perhaps one of the most obvious reasons is a personal interest in letterforms and the desire to experiment with them. Taking the letterforms to the extreme and back and seeking new shapes can even become an obsession. This kind of drive had already flourished in the Czech lands after 1918, when the territory was independent from the Austro-Hungarian Empire and new opportunities became available. New publications, book designs and graphic arts boomed under the umbrella of nationalism and the quest for Czech visual expression. Increasing confidence and the search for national identity enhanced the evolution of Czech book craft along with type design. A small group of artists endeavoured to address the present deficiencies and establish a sovereign Czech style. Names like Vojtěch Preissig, Karel Svolinský, Karel Dyrynk, Jaroslav Benda and later Oldřich Menhart come to mind. They recognized the demand for typefaces to be able to highlight the intrinsic peculiarities of Czech handwriting. A large part of their endeavour was to create balanced diacritics, so crucial for the Czech language.

New fonts for a new era

A similar motivation can be ascribed to the wave of typefaces created after 1990 in the "new" Czech Republic. Not only was there a need to express the freshly gained freedom from the political regime and its visual uniformity, but it also provided tools for the digital era, after photo composition had quickly become obsolete. The majority of the fonts from this era are no longer used. This is irrelevant as they influenced the visual environment and helped to create a distinctly different visual culture from the previous years.

New technologies, such as the introduction of personal computing and the resulting radical change to graphic design and type-making, are good reasons to develop new typefaces. In the case of Eastern Europe, language-specific requirements also came into play. In the early 90s barely any digital typefaces included well-crafted accents. Global markets and necessary language support, together with technological developments, are now more than ever a driving force behind the creation of new fonts. We have high-resolution screens, tablets, e-book readers and many other forms of mobile devices that place new demands on typefaces. Publications tend to exist in both printed and digital format simultaneously with portable devices demanding flexible layouts and brand coherence. Here the typeface has to perform well on all of the different rendering devices without difficulty or adjustment. The best way to ensure this is to create a bespoke typeface. It is, along with the company's logotype and colours, a crucial component of the corporate identity. The typeface communicates with the customer on a subtle but important level, conveying the company's core message and enhancing its recognizability.

Bespoke typefaces

There are several reasons for the growing demand of tailor-made typefaces: they share the same language as the rest of the visual programme of a company, guarantee the process of exchanging information both internally and externally, and allow for the company's expansion with no extra licensing charges. In global markets with their broad diversifications of media, having a distinct typeface can be invaluable. This practice, so common in places like the United States and the United Kingdom, has found its footing in the Czech Republic as well, albeit with some delay and a greater need to convince potential clients. There are good examples in the Czech Republic though, and the creativity of Czech designers and students is still growing and flourishing. Indeed, the growth of independent foundries globally and the fact that mid-sized firms are growing as well are a good indicator for increased appreciation as well as the need for good typography.

Gaining a foothold

For a small foundry, it is important to establish its own unique portfolio of typefaces, ideally with a particular focus, e.g., text typography, scripts or historical revivals. Commercial decisions can lead to the development of new typefaces, and as a small business one needs to respond to and, in the best case scenario, inspire trends within the industry. Quality control and an aim to contribute original solutions rather than plagiaries should be the pillars of new designs. Some of the best solutions are mixtures of personal exploration with an understanding of historical contexts and abstract concepts.

Private interests, technical developments, bespoke client requirements and commercial decisions are all reasons for creating new typefaces. The last item on this list is the preservation and improvement of historical typefaces, which are still relevant today or serve as a direct source for inspiration. There are many grades of authenticity in revivals and it is worth questioning how true one should stay to the original. Typefaces from the 20th century, during hot-metal times, were restricted by the technical requirements of production. For example, italic and bold styles for Linotype machines had to sit on the same widths as the regular style. This lead to "unnatural" shapes, which were a necessary compromise. These concessions can be rectified by reinterpreting the analogue designs and adapting them digitally. From my point of view, revivals have their place and reason, but it is more interesting to develop contemporary ideas.

We can conclude that the five-typeface-credo is a mindset of designers from the 1950s/60s that was rooted in technical limitations as much as ideological ones. It has no place today, and I encourage people to contact type designers and foundries to ask for advice, get additional information and generally involve them at an early stage of the project. Their expertise can help all designers move away from the ordinary and towards originality.

Originally written for the book *TYPO 9010* (see p. 30).

09
Recent noteworthy typefaces

TEXT BY JOHN D. BERRY

TYPEFACE JURY

John D. Berry
Fiona Ross
Jan Middendorp
Indra Kupferschmid
Dan Reynolds
Silvia Sfligiotti
Tamye Riggs
Mark Jamra
Jo De Baerdemaeker
Eben Sorkin
Jean-Baptiste Levée
365typo

Any glance at the compendium of "noteworthy" type designs of 2015 will make it very clear how diverse and unpredictable that list must be. The one thing that is clear about the typographic world of 2015 is that there is no easy, simple summation possible.

There's an easy starting point: the remarkable diversity and variety of sources. This is without any doubt the era of independent type designers. Although we've had a supposed indie era before (and it was fecund indeed), right now we are confronted with the creative anarchy of a type-design community that is in transition, in ferment, and in constant communication with itself.

Trends? All right, we have trends. One of them is the expansion of existing type families into mega-families, or typographic systems, which can (so the theory goes) cope with any typographic problem with one or two or a whole slew of the variations present in the carefully-calibrated system of fonts at your fingertips. Sometimes this really works. Sometimes it doesn't.

Another very obvious development, though it's no longer something unusual, is the proliferation of non-Latin typefaces. The fact that some of the "noteworthy" typefaces of 2015 that were chosen include Armenian, Arabic, and Devanagari is an excellent indication of the range of contemporary type design.

Along with this focus on providing type designs for non-Latin writing systems, there has been strong economic pressure toward developing cross-cultural typographic systems: type families that will (magically) work for branding and identity purposes across several unrelated writing systems. Just look at the type families developed for banks in India to see an example of the challenges, and the solutions, that are possible.

And what's next? No question: creating type families for both print and screen simultaneously. This is very clearly an essential part of typography and type design in the coming years. Since this is becoming the way that graphic designers (i.e., type users) work, it makes sense that type designers would be thinking about both formats (and their many, many variations) at the same time.

10
Buendía

Buendía is an exploration into what a type family can be beyond the traditional suite of progressive weights and widths. The graduation project by César Puertas when he was enrolled in the KABK Type & Media master course, this unique series is structured into six styles with distinct but matching flavours: grotesque, rounded, slab-serif and transitional, all based on the same skeleton. The weights range from thin and medium sans to elegant roman and italic serifs, a cosy bold slab and the extra-beefy rounded sans.

"In Buendía, each member of the family is a different person, not just the same one who gained or lost weight," Puertas says. The series tries to provide as many different design variants as possible within a single concept to give designers a compact but flexible set of options. Nevertheless, all styles have certain features in common, such as closed apertures, swashy tails and curls and slightly curved diagonals. These contribute to a warmth and playfulness that makes Buendía especially suited for packaging design, advertising, books and editorial design.

All styles of Buendía come with an extended Latin character set as well as OpenType features such as small caps, ligatures, and different sets of numerals.

Designer: César Puertas
Foundry: Bold Monday
Release date: October 2015
Country: The Netherlands

GABRIEL JOSÉ DE LA CONCORDIA GARCÍA MÁRQUEZ

EXQUISITELY

▶ *Torta de Choclo is a Fresh Corn Soufflé* ◀

AJIACO SANTAFEREÑO

trädtomat

❾ aguardiente–sugar cane alcohol

tomato & sauces

The cuisine of Colombia consists of a big variety of dishes

City of Medellín

Sabajón is sweet and creamy

GÂTEAU À LA CRÈME

o povo colombiano dá importancia especial ao almoço

EMPANADAS

je pokrm rozšířený ve Španělsku, Portugalsku

A NĚKTERÝCH ZEMÍCH JIŽNÍ Ameriky. Jedná se o zpravidla pšeničnou kapsu plněnou nejčastěji masem (šunkou, tuňákem apod.). Připravuje se v troubě nebo peci. Obzvlášť vyhlášené jsou empanady z Galicie, kde se často plní rybami a mořskými živočichy (mariscos) a přidává se cibule. Namísto drobných kapes se peče velká EMPANADA přes celý plech, z níž se potom odkrajují libovolně velké řezy. V Galicii se dokonce každoročně konají festivaly empanad. Katalánská obdoba pokrmu se nazývá panada.

▶ Die kolumbianischen Empanadas unterscheiden sich nur unwesentlich von denen in den umliegenden lateinamerikanischen Ländern.

Je nach Region und Geschmack findet man Empanadas aus Mais- oder Weizenmehl, meist werden sie in heißem Öl frittiert und gerne zum Kaffee gereicht. In vielen Regionen ist es üblich, neben Hackfleisch die Füllung mit Reis zuzubereiten. Zwiebeln, gekochtes Ei und Hülsenfrüchte, zum Beispiel Erbsen sind ebenfalls beliebt. Gewürzt wird diese Füllung mit comino, der kolumbianischen Variante des Kreuzkümmels. Eine besondere Empanada ist die Empanada de harina pastusa, eine aus Weizenmehl zubereitete Teigtasche, wie sie in Pasto, der Hauptstadt des Deparaments Nariño und ihrer Umgebung serviert wird. Ihre Füllung ist herzhaft mit den zuvor genannten Zutaten, trotzdem wird sie nach dem Frittieren in Kristallzucker gewendet. Diese Mischung aus Salzig und Süß gilt als sehr wohlschmeckend, trotzdem ist sie außerhalb der Region wenig bis gar nicht bekannt und stößt selbst bei Kolumbianern im Allgemeinen auf Misstrauen.

11
Hobeaux

The original Hobo was Art Nouveau-influenced design released in 1910. Over the years, this one-of-a-kind and often maligned typeface slowly degraded with each transition in type technology. In the 1980s, Hobo was one of the first typefaces digitized due mostly to its unique aesthetic and malleable voice. Unfortunately, the care taken in tracing the design left much to be desired, if only because type designers hadn't yet figured out how to best draw curves. Hobo was in desperate need of some attention, but unfortunately got installed on millions of desktop computers as it was. Hobeaux is a modern revival – an attempt to fix the mistakes, and maintain all the glory that made Hobo the powerhouse it was. Each character was redrawn and spaced from scratch. Additionally, descending letters have been provided as stylistic alternates for those seeking a more traditional construction. With five weights and several features for the designer seeking a high performance type family, Hobeaux is a ready and willing addition to any typographic palette. See also p. 51.

Designer: James Edmondson
Foundry: OH no Type Co.
Release date: August 2015
Country: United States

This best-selling guide to decluttering your home from famed Japanese cleaning consultant Marie Kondo takes readers step-by-step through her revolutionary KonMari Method for simplifying, organizing, and storing. Despite constant efforts to declutter your home, do papers still accumulate like snowdrifts and clothes pile up like a tangled mess of noodles? Japanese cleaning consultant Marie Kondo takes tidying to a whole new level, promising that if you properly simplify and organize your home once, you'll never have to do it again. Most methods advocate a room-by-room or little-by-little approach, which doom you to pick away at your piles of stuff forever. **The KonMari Method,** with its revolutionary category-by-category system, leads to lasting results. In fact, none of Kondo's clients have lapsed (and she still has a three-month waiting list). With detailed guidance for determining which items in your house "spark joy" (and which don't), this international best-seller featuring Tokyo's newest lifestyle phenomenon will help you clear your clutter and enjoy the unique magic of a tidy home—and the calm, motivated mindset it can inspire.

12

Adelle Sans Armenian

Adelle Sans Armenian is yet another push in TypeTogether's ongoing multilingual efforts. Adelle Sans, José Scaglione and Veronika Burian's sans-serif counterpart to the award-winning Adelle type family, was expanded to Armenian script with a robust seven weights plus matching italics. It promises to serve Armenian readers well on the web, in print and on screens, and to fill the need for quality Armenian typefaces in editorial use. Careful research and consultation with Armenian type expert Hrant Papazian yielded cultural and typographic consistency within both the Latin and Armenian scripts.

Designers: Veronika Burian & José Scaglione
Foundry: TypeTogether
Release date: November 2015
Country: Czech Republic

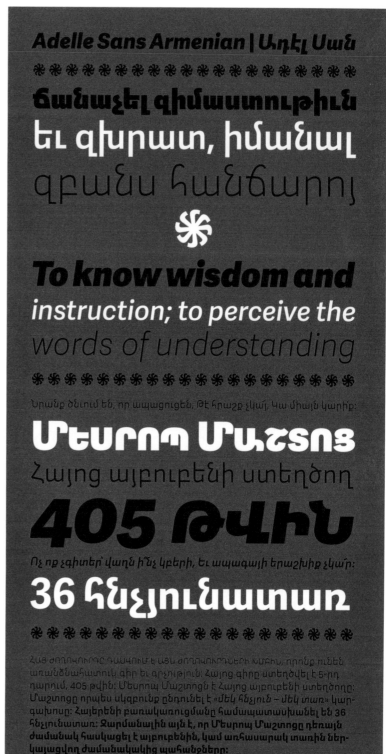

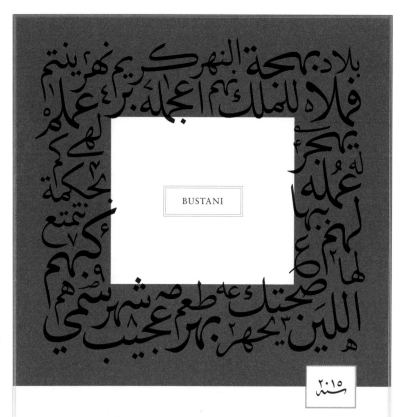

13
Bustani

Naskh is generally considered the primary style for literary text. While it might often appear as one of the simpler cursive styles when seen in its most rationalized typographic interpretations, when it is embraced in its full calligraphic breadth, it has a very rich set of alternative letter shapes with which a calligrapher can choose to compose words and lines of text.

Slowly developed over several years, Bustani is a love letter to the calligraphic naskh style, but is resolutely typographic in its essence. It is a sharply defined interpretation of the flow of the cursive hand, adapted to the regularity of typographic typesetting.

Going beyond Arabic, Persian and Urdu, it is designed to handle fully vocalized text in all the languages that use Arabic script while also meeting the requirements of scholarly manuscripts. See also p. 138.

Designer: Patrick Giasson
Linguistic typographer: Kamal Mansour
Foundry: Monotype
Release date: December 2015
Country: United States

عاد إلى سكونه وجموده في ركنه الذي اضطر إليه ، وقد أخذ لنهار ينصرم والشمس تنحدر إلى مغربها وأخذ يتسرب إلى نفسه شعور شاحب هادئ حزين ، ثم يدعو مؤذن المغرب إلى الصلاة فيعرف الصبي أن الليل قد أقبل ، ويقدر في نفسه أن الظلمة قد أخذت تكتنفه ، ويقدر في نفسه أن لو كان معه في الغرفة بعض المبصرين لأضئ المصباح ليطرد هذه الظلمة المتكاثفة ، ولكنه وحيد لا حاجة له إلى المصباح فيما يظن المبصرون ، وإن كان ليراهم مخطئين في هذا الظن ، فقد كان في ذلك الوقت يفرق تفرقة غامضة بين الظلمة والنور . وكان يجد في المصباح إذا أضئ جليساً له ومؤنساً . وكان يجد في الظلمة وحشة لعلها كانت تأتيه من عقله الناشئ ومن حسه المضطرب ... والغريب أنه كان يجد للظلمة صوتاً يبلغ أذنيه ، صوتاً متصلاً يشبه صوت البعوض لولا أنه غليظ ممتلئ وكان هذا الصوت يبلغ أذنيه فيؤذيها ، ويبلغ قلبه فيملؤه روعاً ، وإذا هو مضطر إلى أن يغير جلسته فيجلس القرفصاء ويعتمد بمرفقيه على ركبتيه ويخفي رأسه بيديه ويسلم نفسه لهذا الصوت الذي يأخذه من كل مكان ...

• من كتاب «الايام» لطه حسين

14
FS Brabo

FS Brabo began to emerge in 2012 while Fontsmith designer Fernando Mello was studying in the Expert Class Type Design course at the Plantin Institute for Typography in Antwerp. His starting point was the genre of 16th century typefaces he had encountered at the Plantin-Moretus Museum, inspired by broad-nibbed calligraphy. The influence of the book-oriented class of garaldes and punch-cutters like Garamond and Granjon are visible in Brabo's proportions.

The contrast in stroke width in FS Brabo, not as pronounced as in typical 16th century fonts, is combined with generous counters to give the family a sturdy, affable character in body text. The serifs are slightly chunkier than the ones found in garaldes, and their sharp cuts and squared edges make them crisp at text sizes. Extravagant ligatures, contextual ending swashes and other stylistic features make FS Brabo colourful and versatile enough for editorial projects, signage, advertising and identities. See also pp. 126 & 147.

Designer: Fernando Mello
Foundry: Fontsmith
Release date: November 2015
Country: United Kingdom

Dalstonist

Surrey Quays to Westminster Bridge Pier

Granjonèsque

MARCOS VALLE, ELIS REGINA & TOM JOBIM

(£1,842 + 325€ = ?!)

Plantin Institute *voor Typografie*

Snapchat

Eastern & Southern Kurdistan

SCHELDEZICHT

Lille Europe

Rua Artur de Azevedo, 32 → Apto. 04

Alfie & Marion

Ponadto większość północnej granicy *Polski* wyznacza

«Eastbourne»

Hydrodynamic
THIN

Morphological
EXTRA LIGHT

Generalization
LIGHT

Southborough
BOOK

Unpredictable
MEDIUM

Checkerboard
BOLD

Inexhaustibly
BLACK

Microbalance
ULTRA

15
Mallory
TEXT BY TOBIAS FRERE-JONES

Mallory began as an experiment in mixing typographic traditions, mapping my own family tree onto typographic history. It was a more personal origin than I had used before: my mother is British and my father was American (and Mallory is my middle name). As I view these typographic traditions, Mallory had to be equally austere and energetic. It was a satisfying challenge and I hoped that users would appreciate the result.

Building type palettes is a critical job for designers, so I also wanted Mallory to combine readily with other typefaces. I used Mallory as a chance to test a long-standing hypothesis of mine: that small sizes in print and text sizes on screen could be treated as essentially the same problem and answer both situations with the same variation, called "MicroPlus".

Designer: Tobias Frere-Jones
Foundry: Frere-Jones Type
Release date: December 2015
Country: United States

COMPARISON OF FLYING MACHINES and ships suggests many points of difference. **Water is a fluid of great density**, with a definite upper surface, on which marine structures naturally rest. A plane in the air may be at any elevation in the surrounding rarefied fluid, and *great attention is required to keep it at the elevation desired*. The air has no surface. The air ship is like a submarine and perhaps rather more safe. An ordinary ship is only partially

BOOK, BOOK ITALIC & BOLD — 9 PT / 13 PT

COMPARISON OF FLYING MACHINES AND SHIPS suggests many points of difference. Water is a fluid of great density, with a definite upper surface, on which marine structures naturally rest. **A plane in the air may be at any elevation in the surrounding rarefied fluid**, and great attention is required to keep it at the elevation desired. The air has no surface. The air ship is like a submarine and perhaps rather more safe. An ordinary ship is only partially immersed; the resistance of the fluid medium is exerted over a portion only of its head end: *but the submarine or the flying machine is wholly exposed to this resistance*. The submarine is subjected to ocean currents of a very few miles per hour, at most; the currents to which the flying machine may be exposed exceed a mile a minute. Put a submarine in the Whirlpool Rapids at Niagara and you

MICROPLUS — 6 PT / 9 PT

16
Modak

Modak is a Devanagari and Latin display typeface with portly curves and thin counters.

It started off as a hand-sketched lettering experiment to test the unexplored possibilities of very heavy, yet legible letterforms in Devanagari. What emerged were plump characters whose curves merge into each other, forming distinct counter shapes.

As we translated the sketches into a functional font, characters were fine-tuned and multiple vowel signs were designed to match precisely with every character. These overlapping vowel signs are a feature unique to Modak. As opposed to a mere composite of two separate glyphs, each conjunct was drawn as a single entity. The challenge was to maintain legibility and consistency across all characters, irrespective of the structural complexity of the script. The resulting typeface is one of its kind and most likely the chubbiest Devanagari typeface to be designed so far.

Designers: Sarang Kulkarni & Maithili Shingre
(Devanagari), Noopur Datye (Latin)
Foundry: Ek Type
Release date: February 2015
Country: India

muffin & tart

बुलबुले गुलगुले चुलबुले चुटकुले

आसमान

100% HAPPINESS

ocean

'sleeping blue whale'

ख़ुशी की पुड़िया!

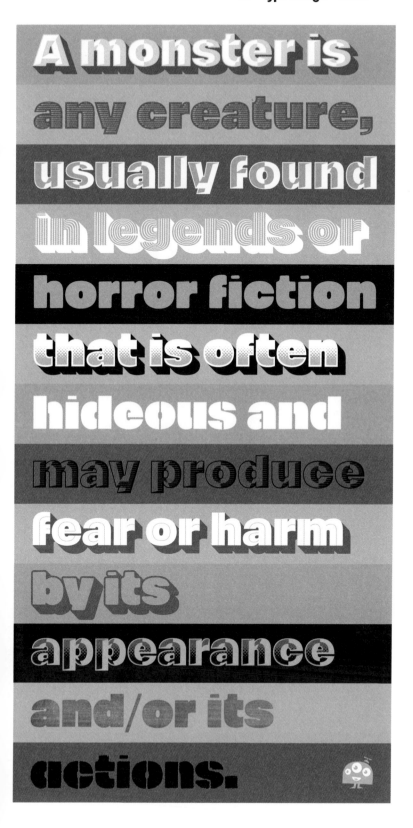

A monster is any creature, usually found in legends or horror fiction that is often hideous and may produce fear or harm by its appearance and/or its actions.

17

Nitti Mostro

Nitti Mostro started its life as the heaviest weight of Nitti Grotesk, optimized for very compact headlines with tight line spacing. To achieve this, ascenders and descenders are kept as short as possible and letter shapes are altered.

While designing this heavy weight, ideas for extra styles popped up and a collection of display typefaces was born. Because some ideas were very complex to draw, Frederik Berlaen was hired to write RoboFont extensions to make the process easier.

The total of eighteen styles are meant to be used extra large and a bit over the top, or at least on top of each other: all styles in the Mostro subfamilies can be layered for multi-coloured and other vibrant effects. The nine cute monster pictograms drawn by Dirk Uhlenbrock are a fun extra.

Because Nitti Mostro lends itself so well for this kind of use, a woodtype version was also made. Samples of prints using the wooden letters can be found on the Bold Monday website.

Designer: Pieter van Rosmalen
Foundry: Bold Monday
Release date: December 2015
Country: The Netherlands

18
Obsidian

Obsidian is a decorative display face containing 1,400 glyphs spanning both roman and italic styles. Inspired by the technological innovations used to create the decorative typefaces of the industrial age, Obsidian uses digital means to achieve a traditional end. When the steel-plate engraving of the 19th century gave rise to a style of ornate lettering, type foundries created intricate printing types to achieve a similar effect. Producing these typefaces required time-consuming hand work, and attempts at mechanization often resulted in "engine-turned" and bland letters. Obsidian is both an homage to this history and an exercise in answering the age-old question of how technology can be used to design ornate, evocative and modern letterforms. To this end, H&Co developed proprietary tools to add highlights to letterforms ultimately creating a suite of software for interpreting two-dimensional letterforms as three-dimensional objects. The result is a majestic type family that honours the traditions of decorative typography while transcending the limitations of the historical style. See also *365typo* No. 1, p. 132.

Designer: Hoefler & Co.
Foundry: Hoefler & Co.
Release date: January 2015
Country: United States

19

Hollie Script

TEXT BY CÉSAR PUERTAS

The crest of the wave of all things hand-made seems to have reached its peak during this decade and both brush-script lettering fonts and a vintage decorative design style could not be more popular.

Hollie Script follows the vintage script trend in type design but sets its own high standard. Starting from its immense character set, the font contains many features that look and feel authentically handwritten or hand-drawn, such as isolated brush strokes and a diversity of exit strokes as alternatives for each letter of the Latin alphabet. It shows that the author, Felipe Calderón, carefully studied several pointed brush models of the past century. In his own words, "Hollie Script is a typeface that pays tribute to all the sign painters and letterers who created amazing work in magazines, walls and windows during the last half of the 20th century."

Hollie Script is especially adequate for setting text in English: many letter combinations and even whole English words were designed separately.

Calderón's work is that of a sign painter in the digital age, and Hollie Script looks and feels convincingly handwritten. In 2015 it was awarded with the Type Directors Club certificate of excellence in type design.

Designer: Felipe Calderón
Foundry: Estudio Calderón
Release date: February 2015
Country: Colombia

20
New type foundries

It's nice to see that a number of the new type foundries that crop up every year still have something surprising in store for us. We picked four that are led by major figures in contemporary type design. The fonts they sell include new interpretations of historical typefaces, fonts used for setting texts in Arabic script-based languages, and "universal" typefaces intended for corporate and commercial use.

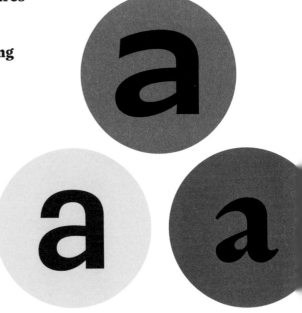

Typotheque Arabic Foundry

Peter Biľak's Typotheque believes that Arabic culture is ready to embrace modern, authentic typefaces, so they created Typotheque Arabic, a new type foundry dedicated to developing original high-quality Arabic typefaces and systems for bilingual typography. The main designer of TPTQ Arabic, Kristyan Sarkis, has been recognized by leading professional bodies and won multiple awards.

Superior Type Foundry

Another new arrival to the family of micro type foundries is Superior Type, founded by Czech type designer Vojtěch Říha, a graduate of the Academy of Arts, Architecture and Design in Prague. The foundry currently offers three type families: the strong, broad, grotesque Hrot in eight different weights; a classical book typeface in four weights named Kunda; and the sans-serif Vegan in six weights.

PANTAC

WILTEI

SABAI

EL RE

FOXI

Zen
Hero
Farm
Frank
Rubrik Edge

Newlyn Type Foundry

The name behind this type foundry is Miles
Newlyn, a world-renowned designer who has
had a hand in designing the logos for Unilever,
Honda, Sky and many more. Together with a small
international team, Newlyn launched the new font
foundry (initially known as TextPrefs) to build
a collection of typefaces that will be the fruit of
20 years' experience creating the typographic
faces and voices of some of the world's biggest
and best businesses.

OH no Type Company

James T. Edmondson launched a brand-new
artisanal type foundry in San Francisco: OH no
Type Company. He landed his company with a
big splash, too, debuting with two typefaces that
overwhelm with awesomeness: Viktor Script and
Hobeaux. The latter, an excellent interpretation of
the oft-mocked Hobo, was very positively received
on social media. In fact, it earned a well-deserved
spot among our top ten typefaces of the year.
See also p. 41.

1

21
The ATF Collection:
Classic American Typefaces Reinterpreted

The American Type Founders Company (ATF) was formed in 1892 as a consolidation of 23 of the most prominent independent type foundries in the United States.

By the early part of the 20th century, ATF dominated the production of metal type for hand-setting in the United States and was at the forefront of technical developments in designing and producing type.

The typefaces originally produced by the American Type Founders Company are well known and well loved. From the familiar sans-serif letterforms seen virtually everywhere to thoughtful revivals of historic text faces, ATF's type designs have inspired countless fonts by other foundries.

Launched in the summer of 2015, the American Type Founders Collection builds on the ATF legacy of originality, creativity and innovation, introducing new interpretations of classic ATF typefaces. Fonts in the ATF Collection are developed with the needs of contemporary type users in mind. Attention to aesthetics and usability are paramount – ATF designer font families build on their predecessors, offering more

weights and widths, as well as robustly expanded character sets and typographic features made possible with digital font technology. The ATF Collection brings the same visual richness to page and screen that handset type once brought to the printed page.

The ATF Collection debuted with ATF Alternate Gothic, ATF Brush, ATF Garamond, ATF Headline Gothic, ATF Poster Gothic, and ATF Wedding Gothic. ATF Railroad Gothic followed in early 2016.

Mark van Bronkhorst, a typeface designer in the San Francisco Bay Area, is the lead designer for the ATF Collection. Working with talented collaborators including Ben Kiel, Alan Dague-Greene, Igino Marini, David Sudweeks and Luis Batlle, Van Bronkhorst will continue to bring the best of American typographic history into the modern world of graphic design.

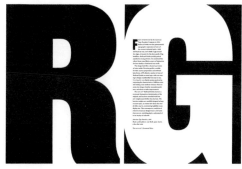

1 – ATF Brush promotional notecard and sparkle toothbrush distributed at TypeCon 2015.
Creative: Justin Flood. Photo: Robbie Augspurger
2 – Introductory spread from ATF Railroad Gothic specimen

2

איפה היית בוסדרי ארץ

The story behind the design of Hadassah Hebrew typeface revolves around three countries and almost three decades.

2/5 .ה טודזל נבר.

22
Hadassah Hebrew typeface goes digital, legally

TEXT BY LIRON LAVI TURKENICH

In the early 1930s, while working for Offizin Haag-Drugulin in Leipzig, Henri Friedlaender was asked by the Schocken publishing house to design a new Hebrew typeface. He undertook this challenge with the intention of designing a good modern Hebrew typeface, unlike the existing options of that time. This allegedly simple goal was significant in a time where the norm was of low-quality Hebrew types and dominating sans-serif styles.

Friedlaender wished to draw letterforms that were rooted in the past but designed for the present. He was after simple forms, extracted from his analysis of existing letter structures. Throughout the process he was fully engaged with discovering a proper evolution from Hebrew written forms into type used in printing.

The first stages of the design were fully interlaced with visual research into historic Hebrew letterforms. It is no wonder that he chose to find influences in several sources such as manuscripts and Rudolf Koch's work. Hadassah's strength and innovation lay in its unique combination of two calligraphic styles, Sepharadic and Ashkenazic.

Friedlaender saw the importance of designing a whole text family rather than a single weight, and therefore simultaneously drew a regular weight, bold weight and italics. In the end, the italics were not produced, nor was a later suggestion for a condensed version that would be used in newspapers.

When Friedlaender left Germany for the Netherlands in 1932, he continued to work on the typeface even without a client, driven by his own curiosity. As the design progressed, the letters grew more and more stable, becoming one coherent typeface that managed to achieve movement and rhythm.

Before casting Hadassah typeface at Lettergieterij Amsterdam, Friedlaender and the foundry were unsure how the public would accept the new typeface. Hadassah was finally released in 1958, 27 years after the first sketch was drawn, and it quickly became popular.

In 2009, Fridlaender's family sued Masterfont type foundry in Israel for years of selling Hadassah typeface licences illegally and treating it as if they owned the rights. Litigation ended in 2015 and brought this saga to a happy end: Friedlaender's family was compensated and a new and adequate digital version of Hadassah typeface was released. This version was the work of Yanek Iontef, approved and encouraged by the family. After many decades and several technologies to which Hadassah was adapted, it is finally possible to digitally set text in this important typeface.

ההתחלות של אות

הדסה

מקורן בתקופה בה תהו מחדש

על הצורה והתפקיד

מההכתב

(Bauhaus) לנסים

הראשון באות פוטורה Futura ולהופעת הספר

Neue Typographie

לִבְלְבוּ הַשָּׁטִים לְנֶגְדְּךָ וְזָלְפוּ

בְּאַפְּךָ בְּשָׂמִים, וְצִיצֵיהֶן חֵצִים

23
Experiment rewarded: Manuel Guerrero

TEXT BY FEIKE DE JONG

When Manolo Guerrero sent in his work to the Type Director's Club in 2009, the judges set it aside as irrelevant. Obviously some designer in Mexico had not quite understood that this was a type design competition, while this work only presented isometric textures. Only after an hour of contemplating the equidistant lines before them did the letters emerge before the judges' eyes, spelling out a tongue twister in Spanish.

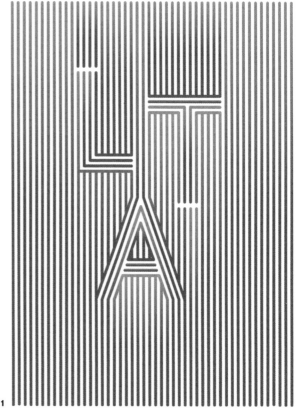

1

1 – Cover image for the RGB Magazine, Mexico
2 – Poster for the design conference Passion
& Design V Puebla, Mexico, 2014
3 – The Lucky One. Silkscreen poster made for
The Druck Berlin Screenprint Festival, 2015
4 – Poster to protest over missing 43 students in
Mexico, 2014
5 – Poster to celebrate the 50th anniversary of Félix
Beltrán, 2013
6 – Julian Carrillo's Thirteen Sounds. Self
interpretation, 2015

ILUSTRACIÓN: ELY ELY | ARTE OBJETO: FANNGORA
TIPOGRAFÍA: **MANOLO GUERRERO** | CARTEL: **ELMER SOSA**
DISEÑO SOCIAL: MICHAL BATORY | DISEÑO INDUSTRIAL: MASISA LAB
DISEÑO E INNOVACIÓN: **CARMINA SANTOS** | AUDISEÑO: TONY IRAGORRI
http://www.pasionydiseno.com

PASIÓN & DISEÑO
23.24.25.
OCT.

2

"I am interested in the frontier between abstract form and the meaningful letter form. For me, experimentation in typography means discarding the functionality of the letter and privileging new techniques and expression," commented Guerrero from his studio in the Mexican provincial capital of San Luis Potosí.

This approach saw itself rewarded once more with the silver medal for poster design in the A' Design Awards in April 2016. Guerrero's work is inspired by the 1960s and 1970s Op Art of Victor Vasarely and Bridget Riley and designers such as Niklaus Troxler and Felix Beltran. But it is also part of the strong poster design scene in San Luis Potosí that has evolved around the design courses at the Universidad Autonoma de San Luis Potosí, where Guerrero is a professor. This prize adds another medal to the awards

cabinet at Bluetypo in San Luis, the design studio where Guerrero works with his partner Erendida Mancilla.

Guerrero's work is not only an outstanding Mexican example of the expanding worldwide interest in three-dimensional type design; his experimental inclinations have extended from optical to auditory with another font, Sonotipo, in which the letters react to sound. Sonotipo has been used in experimental music concerts locally and have been selected for the 2016 edition of Tipos Latinos. See also p. 144.

AYOTZINAPA 2014

COMPARTE, IMPRIME, HABLA Y DISCUTE

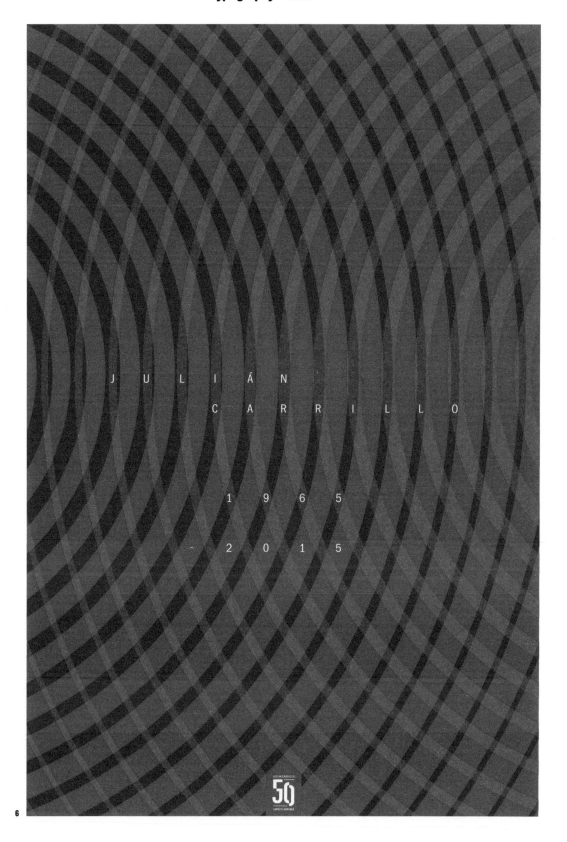

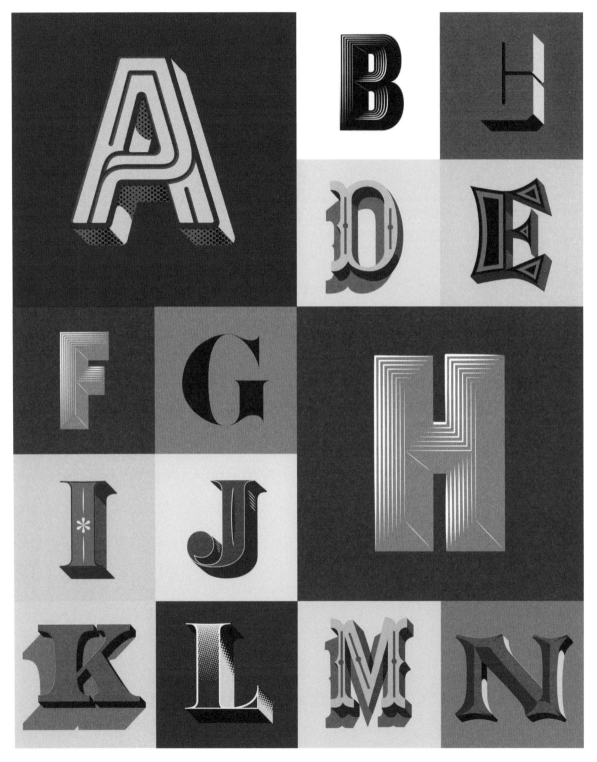

7 – 36 Days of Type is a project of restless creativity, where participants are challenged to design a letter or number each day, resulting in an outcome of the ability to represent the same symbol from many different perspectives. This project ran with the hashtag #36daysoftype on Instagram. For the 3rd edition Manuel Guerrero designed a poster with each letter that he posted during the 36 days, printed in serigraph form by Arturo Negrete.

alphabettes

Alphabettes

alphabettes

alphabettes

ALPHABETTES

ऐल्फाबॉड्ड

ALPHABETTES

الفابتس

alphabettes

Alphabettes

Alphabettes

АЛФАВЕТЫ

alphabettes

24
Alpha females in type:
Alphabettes

TEXT BY INDRA KUPFERSCHMID

It was sort of in the air in the summer of 2015. Several rounds of Twitter discussions about too few women speaking at conferences and the lack of female participation on occasionally harsh-seeming type fora sparked a series of emails on August 10 about bringing together the women in type.

As the emails became too numerous, we moved to a handier venue. This was the incidental birth of *Alphabettes* – a name we decided on in two minutes without much thought or consensus on how to actually pronounce it. Some say Alpha-bet-tes, some say Alpha-betts. (That Google announced their umbrella company Alphabets that very same night passed totally unnoticed by me.)

Alphabettes is a loose international network of women working in type, typography and the lettering arts. We grew rapidly in no time – by January 2017 we numbered 175 members – and we also quickly stirred up some much needed discussion. However, the main idea is to provide a platform to showcase our work, publish our ideas and research, help each other professionally, and just generally make the many women who work in the field more visible. It's not that we haven't been around all this time, we just weren't as blazing loud on our own.

To facilitate this, we launched our own site at alphabettes.org just one month later, publishing just about everything type-related that interested any one of us (each article represents the views of the author, not the entire group). The topics range from news, interviews, research on linguistics or type casting, to design work, reviews, instructive videos and reports from events. Three highlights so far have included the "Letter Love" series in February 2016 featuring daily posts about type-related ephemera dear to our hearts, "Our favourite typefaces of 1915" and the launch of a mentorship program open to everyone starting out in our industry.

Not all members of the group are active in the same way and intensity. Some blog, some help in the background, some focus on outreach activities, while others are just there with us in spirit. The biggest gain and impact for me personally is that we have all learned about so many new people we didn't have on our radar before. And the most important thing for me about the site is that it's first and foremost an interesting place to publish and read about typography, that just happens to be run by women.

25
Ten women type designers

TEXT BY DR. SHELLEY GRUENDLER

Typography has never been more prevalent or more trendy. People are finally noticing that there is far more to letterforms than the drop-down font menu on a computer screen.

This rapid growth in awareness coincides with widespread screen-based technology and a burgeoning typographic education industry, both of which have allowed more people to learn about, and participate in type design.

Type designers create the letterforms that typographers, graphic designers and everyday people use. Note that type designers are typographers, but typographers are not necessarily type designers. To be a type designer one needs acute attention to detail, an innovative creative eye and meticulous diligence to apply a concept through all possible micro-permutations, some of which might require years.

I asked each designer about their "alternate careers", that is, what they would be doing if typography didn't exist. Asking people this question, typographers in particular, can often reveal more about the typography industry than the person who answered. Many of the designers mentioned here have similar alternate careers. Most mention linguistics, product design or research, signifying similar analytical thinking related to language.

These type designers demonstrate a range of specializations, backgrounds and interests. Limiting this article to only ten women was difficult and truly a wonderful problem to have today.

Originally published in *Adobe Create Magazine*.

Sara Soskolne
Laura Worthington
Pooja Saxena
Victoria Rushton
Ksenya Samarskaya
Veronika Burian
Marina Chaccur
Nina Stössinger
Liron Lavi Turkenich
Nicole Dotin

Sara Soskolne

Canada / United States

Sara Soskolne has perhaps one of the most coveted type design jobs in the world: Senior Type Designer at Hoefler & Co. She has co-produced some of the most popular typefaces of the past decade, including Gotham, Tungsten and Sentinel.

She began her career as a graphic designer in Canada, where she became increasingly fixated on typography. After ten years she moved to England to earn her Masters in Type Design from the University of Reading. Soskolne states that the complexity of type design is what attracted her and she wanted to apply her "fastidious tendencies" to it. She remains interested in linguistics and how multiscript languages function.

One of Soskolne's most notable workplace collaborations is the impeccable Quarto. It has a memorable historical voice, nearly a Didone, yet it remains versatile and applicable for modern use. Quarto is yet another example of how Soskolne's visual thinking has affected how many people throughout the world see language.

ALTERNATE CAREER: Linguistics

There is *nothing* simple or **dull** in achieving the transparent page. *Vulgar ostentation* is twice as easy as **discipline.**

Quarto by Hoefler & Co.

WE ARTISTS DO NOT THINK — WE FEEL!

Within lie hundreds of rooms

THE FICKLENESS OF RICH MEN WHO HATE TO READ

Beatrice Warde

Adorn by Laura Worthington

Laura Worthington
United States

Laura Worthington is one of the most prolific type designers today. She releases extensive families that are useful for a variety of graphic design applications, such as Charcuterie.

Her background is in calligraphy, which she learned while growing up in Portland, Oregon. Worthington maintains that it is the building of a design system that interested her in type design. She is fascinated with the process of encouraging type to function in a manner similar to handwriting and lettering.

Her range, rooted so extensively in hand lettering, is astonishingly diverse and her specialty is cheerful scripts with flirty swoops and loops. Ed's Market has a relaxed sign painter's vibe, Voltage perfectly recreates early 20th-century advertising scripts, and Al Fresco is quite dignified and airy. But don't always expect "pretty" from Laura, for she then surprises you with spiky Sepian and creepy Grindelgrove. In the time it took you to read this, she has probably already completed a new typeface. Or two. Or three.

ALTERNATE CAREER: Product design

Pooja Saxena
India

Pooja Saxena attempted her own type design projects while earning her Communication Design degree in Delhi, India. She describes them as naïve, but I find them energetic. It didn't take long for her to realize that she wanted much more for her letterforms. She received her Master's Degree in Type Design at the University of Reading and followed it with a typographic internship at Apple, where she learned about large-scale projects as well as collaborative type design teams.

She was drawn to type design through her interest in languages, and often practices writing them in the manner in which a child would learn. New scripts intrigue her while she figures out how the language works, but then promptly frustrate her as she "explores the shaping behaviours" while progressing towards the detailed design stage.

Farsan, one of her multi-script typefaces, has a welcoming feel with numerous potential applications. This mono-linear sans serif has a narrow body, slightly rounded terminals and clever crossbars (the overshoot on the R, A and H is adorable). Saxena's comfort with scripts is evident in the seemingly simple, yet quite complex stacking of diacritical marks in Vietnamese. Even the Gujarati has an organized rhythm, yet the stroke still has fun bends and flicks.

ALTERNATE CAREER: Linguistics

bear with me this long-winded and fragrant metaphor

એક પુસ્તક માંથી છાપેલ

વાઇન ઇજ સો સ્ટ્રેંજ એન્ડ પોટેન્ટ અ થિન્ગ

transparent or invisible

printing is meant to convey specific and coherent ideas

Farsan by Pooja Saxena

Victoria Rushton
United States

Victoria Rushton was an Illustration major in college until she took a graphic design class. She discovered that type design in particular was the best direction for her, and the remainder of her illustration classes suffered as a result.

Rushton quickly registered for a type design class, where she began working on the typeface that would become Marcia. She remarks that she doesn't expect anyone to see these letterforms as she does, for the typeface symbolizes her journey from nothing to something and she takes solace in knowing that the next font will always be better. When she sees Marcia, she sees the bad ideas, redraws and subsequent fixes along with the resulting learning, practice and success.

Upon graduating she started to work at FontBureau, where she has learned even more on the job. Rushton states that she likes to make things with a purpose, what she calls "things that have jobs", which lends itself exactly to her profession. She says that the core of type design is a considered need, while contextual beauty is a secondary concern. Rushton has an ardent interest in the significance of written communication and views her role as a type designer as a manner in which "to contribute to the words we're lucky enough to share with each other".

ALTERNATE CAREER: Journalist

first chose

THE MOST EXQUISITE LIMITED EDITIONS

simple set of ideas

A STAINED-GLASS WINDOW OF MARVELOUS BEAUTY, BUT A FAILURE AS A WINDOW

it is the transparent goblet again!

Marcia by Victoria Rushton

THE MAZE

because no cloud must come between your eyes and the fiery heart of the liquid

YOUR WILDEST INGENUITY

beautiful thing

SPEND ENDLESS YEARS of HAPPY EXPERIMENT in DEVISING that CRYSTALLINE GOBLET which is WORTHY

Wyeth by Ksenya Samarskaya

Ksenya Samarskaya
Russia / United States

Ksenya Samarskaya is a Renaissance woman, with typography being the most recent application of her diverse interests and background. She has studied the Fine Arts and the Sciences and found infinite connections between them.

She learned type design while working at Hoefler & Frere-Jones, applying her wide-ranging aesthetic and technical skills. Samarskaya had never expected to pursue type design, but the unexpected path fit well into her ideas regarding communication, culture, translation and form. Since founding her own studio, she has since consulted with the top foundries in the world on multi-script typography.

Typographers appeal to Samarskaya, as they tend to have broad knowledge with deep interests in the field along with a touch of boldness (yes, pun intended). In her professional studio, Samarskaya expands her focus to include brand messaging, which depends heavily on typography that is often customized. The manner in which typography facilitates connections, along with its ubiquity, is what keeps her interested day to day and year to year.

ALTERNATE CAREER: Micronations

Veronika Burian

Czech Republic / Spain

Veronika Burian was a product designer in Italy when she learned Fontlab from a colleague and was instantly hooked. Burian then earned a Master's in Type Design from the University of Reading, which she followed with several years as a professional type designer at Dalton-Maag. She then launched the extremely successful independent type foundry TypeTogether with a colleague from her Master's program, José Scaglione, currently President of the Association Typographique Internationale. Type-Together is constantly reaping industry awards – and rightly so, as they make the profession appear effortless.

Burian is impressed by the magnitude by which our environment is affected by visual language, specifically how letterforms can affect culture, information and organization. Her typefaces are designed with a function in mind, and you will see it in perfect applications in newspapers, magazines and books all over the world. You have most certainly seen her work, Abril, Adelle and the all-pervasive Bree with that noticeably cheeky k, g, and y. See also p. 36.

ALTERNATE CAREER: Photography or dance

(thought transference)

It is sheer magic

THAT I SHOULD BE ABLE TO HOLD A ONE-SIDED CONVERSATION

by means of black marks on paper

WITH AN UNKNOWN PERSON HALF-WAY ACROSS THE WORLD.

Crete by Veronika Burian

You may choose your own favorite

VINTAGE

for this imaginary demonstration,

so that it be a deep shimmering crimson in color.

Chic by Marina Chaccur

Marina Chaccur

Brazil / The Netherlands

Marina Chaccur first earned a graphic design degree in Brazil before moving to England to get her Graphic Design MA. After working as a designer, design instructor, hand letterer and letterpress printer, she realized that she wanted more and traveled back to Europe for the Type Media MA at KABK.

Chaccur is an excellent example of a person striving to absorb as much as possible in as many places as possible with as many people as possible in a short amount of time. Her education was just as much outside of the classroom as in it, as she enrolled in professional typographic workshops while attending numerous typography and design conferences around the world.

There are only a few type designers today with such extensive experience in handlettering, type design and letterpress printing, and Chaccur is one of these elite. She says that she

revels in the systematic thinking of type design and it remains an excellent outlet for her admittedly perfectionist tendencies. Her typeface Chic (typemedia2011.com/marina), created with the idea of dressing letterforms in a fashionable manner, is staggering in scope. It has readable text weights and sumptuous Didone displays. Through intertwining swirls of the ornamented letterforms, Chaccur effortlessly brings the Rococo era into today's world.

ALTERNATE CAREER: Fashion or interior design

Nina Stössinger
Switzerland / The Netherlands

Nina Stössinger was a graphic design student in Germany with a focus on multimedia studies when her interest in typography developed. After graduating she joined a postgraduate type design class in Zurich as she wanted to learn about it but didn't know where to start. Stössinger says that she read a lot, made a lot and looked at a lot of type, all of which eventually lead her to the Type Media Program at KABK in the Netherlands.

She articulates that she loves the "crossroads of intersecting interests" that type design entails, between "form and language, writing and drawing, technology and media, psychology and physiology, and culture and history". As with other type designers, Stössinger enjoys the difficulties and the complexities as it keeps her interested and shall do so for years yet to come.

Her typeface Ernestine was well received for its charm, usefulness and friendly feel. However, her new yet-to-be-released chunky typeface, Nordvest, is equally amicable. It has a strong horizontal axis and still retains a bit of sass in unexpected places, such as the jaunty k or the hints of humanism in the italic r and v.

ALTERNATE CAREER: Video editing (it's just like kerning pairs)

so strange and potent

THE VIRTUES OF THE PERFECT WINEGLASS

❋❋ *a thousand mannerisms*

capable of stirring and altering men's minds

COLOURLESS

Nordvest by Nina Stössinger

האזן לשיר (song) בשפה שאתה לא מבין

ㄥፘፘ፩ קסם magic

the one clue that can guide you through the maze

inside the room

 መፅ ኢፎ፦ሳኔ ስ፣ፘ፫ የ፦ስ፬ חובב טיפוגרפיה לוקח עמוד מודפס

Makeda by Liron Lavi Turkenich

Liron Lavi Turkenich
Israel

Liron Lavi Turkenich first earned a Bachelor's of Design in Visual Communication in Tel Aviv. She followed this with an internship at a local typographer, which cemented her interest in the field, and then promptly traveled to the University of Reading for the Type Design Master's degree.

Through typography, Lavi Turkenich discovered an outlet for her detailed focus, prolonged patience and interest in comprehensive research. She views each typeface as a journey, filled with intensive learning.

She is constantly captivated with letterforms and how intrinsic they are to our daily lives. As an example, Lavi Turkenich became interested in Amharic because of the discrepancy between the large amount of Ethiopians that live in Israel and the lack of printed documents and typefaces available in their script.

But it is how different scripts interact, how they influence and are influenced, that interests her the most. In Israel, multiple scripts are used and viewed together, and she wanted to create a type family that did the same.

Makeda, Lavi Turkenich's type design that deftly combines Arabic and Hebrew, started from such an offhand idea and grew into a harmonic functional face. See also p. 54.

ALTERNATE CAREER: Food critic, weaver, linguist, travel writer, speech therapist, archivist, producer

window

OUR SUBCONSCIOUSNESS IS ALWAYS AFRAID OF BLUNDERS

THE MENTAL EYE

swaggering up and down the streets of Paris

marvelous

Pique by Nicole Dotin

Nicole Dotin
United States

Nicole Dotin was a practicing graphic designer before she transitioned into typography. Once she completed the Type Design Master's program at the University of Reading, she became a professional type designer at Process Type Foundry. She states that the intrinsic nature of the method of type design is what drew her to the profession; the independent nature of type design is an added bonus.

One of her most notable typefaces, Pique, is filled with personality with its puffy thicks and angular thins, and still maintains an exceptionally even rhythm. Equally distinctive is that fabulous flippy connecting stroke that is just as seductive ending words as when it connects them. Pique has a vibrant voice, a difficult task when creating a fluid typographic system that can often anesthetize the more humanist strokes.

ALTERNATE CAREER: Scientific research or antiques

26
100 years of Johnston

TEXT BY CATHERINE DIXON & PHIL BAINES

2

One hundred years after its first appearance on London's underground railway networks, Edward Johnston's "block letter" alphabet is being celebrated for the contribution it has made not only to the visual language of sans-serif typeface design, but also the visual identity of Transport for London and the city itself. [1]

3

4

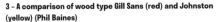

3 – A comparison of wood type Gill Sans (red) and Johnston (yellow) (Phil Baines)
4 – The original Johnston still in use. The bullseye already existed – perhaps created by Harry Ford of the District Railway – but Edward Johnston gave it the definitive form it would have until the 1960s. (Phil Baines)
5 – New Johnston (grey) and Johnston 100 (red) compared (Courtesy Monotype)
6 – In 1919–20 Johnston also designed two condensed alphabets (2" & 5") to be used alongside his standard "block letters" on bus destination blinds. (Central Lettering Record)

Johnston came to London in 1898 after an abortive career in medicine. There he met W. R. Lethaby, architect and founding Principal of the Central School of Arts & Crafts who saw something in his tentative lettering work and offered him a teaching position a year later. Johnston's combination of historical observation and practical application of its lessons formed the basis for his teaching, first at the Central from 1899, and later at many other institutions.

Johnston's work for the Underground Group[2] came about through an introduction by Gerard Meynell of the Westminster Press to Frank Pick, Commercial Manager. Pick wanted a "block letter" alphabet to unify the appearance of publicity material. The result was Johnston's "ordinary" (equivalent to regular or medium) alphabet from 1916, comprising capitals based on the proportions of

Roman Square Capitals as seen on the inscription of the Trajan Column. Johnston was not absolutely dogmatic in this, so the widths of E and F are wider – more like Caslon, which was a typeface he was very familiar with – and the M is more Florentine, avoiding the heavy massing that a more Roman form would suggest. His lowercase follows the pattern of his Foundational Hand, which is based on the script in the Ramsey Psalter – a central model in his teaching. The heavy weight, for capitals and numerals only, was not added until 1929; the proportions of the "ordinary's" x-height made a heavy lowercase impossible and it was not pursued.

The alphabets were originally supplied as printed sheets to act as a guide to lithographic artists preparing artwork, but the designs were quickly converted to wood and metal type with the resulting Johnston typeface

generally identified as being the first "Humanist" sans given its visual pedigree.

It took time for the role of the "typeface as identity" to evolve. Lettering was already a feature of many stations, and use of the new alphabet for station names and signage or as part of a company house style did not start to happen in any systematic way until the early 1920s.

Out with the old, in with the new
By the 1970s Johnston's limitations of just having two weights and being available in only wood and metal type proved a threat to its ongoing use. In 1979 the design consultancy Banks & Miles suggested that they revisit Johnston with a view to generating a new and more flexible three-weight typeface family with italics and condensed variants. The detailed work for this was entrusted to Eiichi Kono,

6

5

Mind the gap

and the result was the typeface New Johnston. As Kono himself credited the difference between old and new, Johnston's "block letter" represented "the original masterpiece, whereas the new one provided up-to-date functionality".[3]

That functionality has endured with New Johnston having been in use ever since. Until now, that is. As we write, Monotype has just launched Johnston100, commissioned by Transport for London to meet the demands of new digital environments with all the necessary refinements and character sets that entails. The opportunity was also taken to re-introduce some of Johnston's original quirks, albeit to the enlarged x-height of Kono's New Johnston.

One thing is clear: 100 years on it would seem certain that our affection for these letterforms will endure yet. Happy birthday, Johnston.

1 Among the celebrations held: the Sussex village in which Johnston was living as part of a thriving community of artists / practitioners when he drew the typeface hosted the exhibition *Underground: 100 years of Edward Johnston's lettering for London* at the Ditchling Museum of Art + Craft on 12 March through 11 September 2016; Johnston's endeavours were celebrated at Central Saint Martins with a display titled *100 years of Johnston's block letter alphabet for the Underground Group* on 19 March till 24 April 2016; and the London Transport Museum has marked the centenary with a two-year programme of tours, talks and events under the umbrella title *Johnston Journeys*.
2 In 1916 the Underground Group was the largest, but not the only, underground railway company. It covered only a part of today's much more extensive network. In 1933 all companies were merged as London Transport, which is now part of Transport for London.
3 Eiichi Kono. 2003. "New Johnston", *Pen to Printer* no. 8 (Journal of the Edward Johnston Foundation), pp. 36–42.

27
Reissue of the 1975 NASA Graphic Standards Manual

TEXT BY JAKUB SKALICKÝ

When you look at the graphically pure NASA logo, still progressive even forty years after it was created, it's a bit difficult to understand why you can't find them on spaceships anymore. The story of the rise, development and fall of one of the symbols of 1970s graphic design is told in the superbly narrated reissue of NASA's original graphic design manual.

In 1972 the United States government launched the Federal Design Improvement Program, a series of grants allowing government departments to hire architects and designers who could supply better-looking desks and reports. NASA was high up on the list, and a Request for Proposals went out in 1974. A tiny studio named Danne & Blackburn also submitted a proposal – and their submission was, one would think, a long shot. Their firm was very small, without the cachet of Vignelli Associates or Push Pin Studios, the Eames Office or any of the other prominent design shops of the era. It was barely a year old and they had only three employees. But its two partners, Richard Danne and Bruce Blackburn, knew what they were doing: Danne had been doing (among other things) a lot of Paramount movie posters, including a superb one for *Rosemary's Baby* in 1968.

The primary objective was to make a case for replacing the NASA insignia (the "Meatball") with a more useful new logotype. The "Meatball" was complicated, hard to reproduce and laden with comic-book imagery.

Photos: Brian Kelley

Goodbye Meatball, hello Worm

Danne & Blackburn knew that the new logo should be progressive, versatile, readable at a great distance and easy to reproduce. Something terribly simple and clean. Some anchor. That something came out of Blackburn's pen – a monochrome logo with a single-width stroke, constructed of just three compound-curve lines. It was bold, like NASA itself; it was technological in its swoop. The two capital As lacked crossbars, suggesting rocket nose cones or the shock waves that those nose cones produced.

The first presentation was made in the autumn of 1974. And – for the employees of the agency – it started with a little shock: the mandatory black or blue colour was replaced with a solid orangey-red corresponding to Pantone 185. The colour was an unusual choice, but one that Danne & Blackburn believed in. Airlines and military agencies tended to go with blue logos, suggesting the sky, sea and coolness; they instead chose to convey action and heat. It was a real challenge to beat this and various other visual stereotypes, but

they did it. They probably won the contest with their add-on, which was not required in the NASA contract: a comprehensive, coordinated communication system. Their bid was not just another ornamental badge to be stuck on products by personnel and sub-contractors; these supporting visuals made the Program "real" and convincing.

The new logotype, which quickly earned the moniker "the Worm" from traditionalists shortly after its launch, soon found itself not only in print, but also on rocket fuselages, wings of

tive, wasteful through duplication of effort and account for inconsistent and fragmented communications.

In 1975, NASA introduced its Unified Visual Communication System. Similar to any systematic approach, it was developed to save time and money; further, the system has allowed our internal design staff to improve the overall quality of NASA's graphic materials.

The System is based on functional considerations and provides for simplicity of production and clarity in communications. By instituti Unified Visual Communication System we NASA, have been able to benefit in many w Substantial Cost Savings–

Because of the standardization, significant omies have been realized in the production materials.

Man-hours reduced–

With a systems approach, time previously devoted to decision-making on many proje become unnecessary with the advent of sys

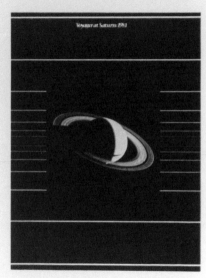

This high-quality, 4-color publication specifically features the Voyager project while adhering, in spirit, to the graphics standards. In publications of this sort the NASA identification would appear on the outside back cover.

Camera-read pre-assemble an exact conf information (i Agency title, tification and a number of s the art ensure high-quality r of the NASA s Repro art rep of the single l saving eleme system.

4

nning and operating guidelines.
proved Productivity–
using established working grids and standard
mats, less time is needed to organize the lay-
of a publication.
eater Efficiency Overall–
mmunication between managers initiating
s and the design staff producing the jobs is
atly streamlined since many of the
iables have been eliminated by the system.
e, Unified Organization–

Continuity in graphic design reinforces the
total Agency, and repetition of the NASA design
attitude achieves greater retention.
An Organization-Wide Policy–
With one set policy, confusion is all but eliminated and the policy promotes efficiency and
clarity in all communications.

aging developed to
audio tapes and
eels which are sent
broadcast media
rates how the
ics standards apply
ee-dimensional
. By using the sys-
the packages clearly
fy the material as
ng from NASA.

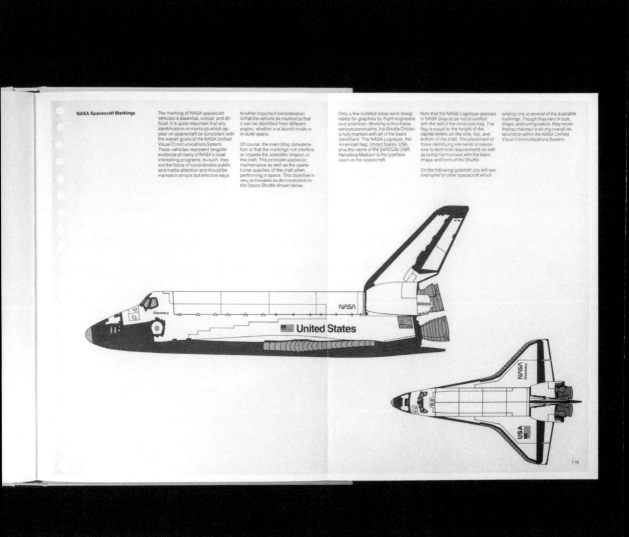

NASA Spacecraft Markings

The marking of NASA spacecraft vehicles is essential, critical, and difficult. It is quite important that any identification or markings which appear on spacecraft be consistent with the overall goals of the NASA Unified Visual Communications System. These vehicles represent tangible evidence of many of NASA's most interesting programs. As such, they are the focus of considerable public and media attention and should be marked in simple but effective ways.

Another important consideration is that the vehicle be marked so that it can be identified from different angles, whether in a launch mode or in outer space.

Of course, the overriding consideration is that the markings not interfere or impede the scientific mission of the craft. This principle applies to maintenance as well as the operational qualities of the craft when performing in space. This objective is very achievable as demonstrated on the Space Shuttle shown below.

Only a few isolated areas were designated for graphics by flight engineers and scientists. Working within these serious constraints, the Shuttle Orbiter is fully marked with all of the basic identifiers: The NASA Logotype, the American flag, United States, USA, plus the name of the particular craft. Helvetica Medium is the typeface used on the spacecraft.

Note that the NASA Logotype appears in NASA Gray so as not to conflict with the red of the American flag. The flag is equal to the height of the capital letters on the side, top, and bottom of the craft. The placement of these identifying elements is responsive to technical requirements as well as being harmonious with the basic shape and form of the Shuttle.

On the following gatefold you will see examples of other spacecraft which

employ one or several of the available markings. Though they vary in size, shape, and configuration, they nevertheless maintain a strong overall relationship within the NASA Unified Visual Communications System.

space shuttles, and all sorts of aircraft and rovers. It wouldn't be far from the truth to place it among the sources of inspiration for George Lucas' Star Wars brand.

Perhaps surprisingly, though, some of the same people who spent their days designing titanium nose cones and integrated circuits preferred to spend their evenings in houses built along neo-Colonial lines instead of ones made of glass and steel. There was also a noticeable (and understandable) generational divide: The younger NASA employees liked the

new logo, and the older ones, by and large, did not.

Goodbye Worm, hello Meatball

If the early 1970s had been the zenith of modern design, the early 1990s were the peak of postmodernism. Pop culture was referenced cut up, and reshaped, sometimes to the point of absurd incoherence. When Dan Goldin took the helm at NASA in 1992, suddenly things started to break down for the Worm. In the spirit of "a new broom sweeps clean", changes came to the organization – starting with the

logo. Not a new logo corresponding to the times, though. To save money, the decision was made to resurrect James Modarelli's Meatball from 1958.

Over the next few years, the Worm was stripped from printed material, signage and everything else. Stories abound at NASA about the frantic scrubbing of the Worm from any building or office that Goldin was about to visit, and about his irritation whenever he'd run across one that hadn't been removed.

When it is rendered well, the Meatball tells a story and provides

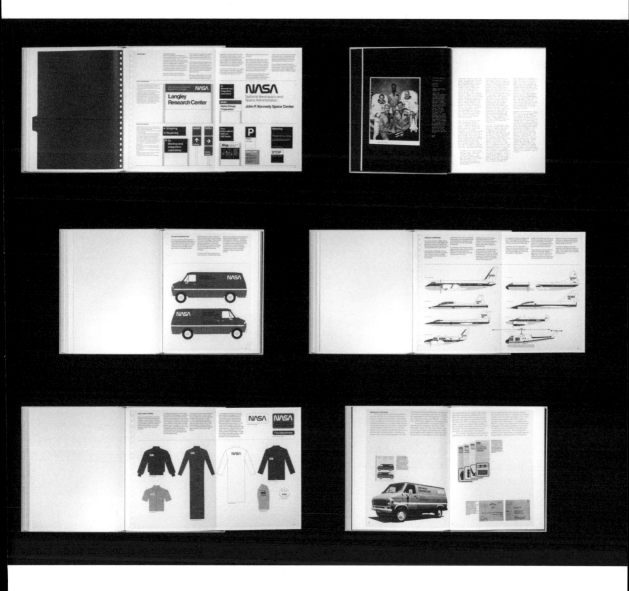

continuity. But it's hard to argue, from a design standpoint, that it's really better than the Worm. The Worm is forever modern; the Meatball, despite its charms, never will be. For an agency whose mission is so thoroughly directed at the future, a retro emblem is an eccentric choice at best. Could there be one more reversal ahead? Given the cost it's unlikely, but it's also not impossible to imagine. To the post-postmodern eye, the Worm looks a lot cooler and less dated than it did when Dan Goldin cast his eye upon it that day at Langley; the Meatball, by contrast, looks increasingly like kitsch, and the starry speckles in the background mean that it reproduces badly on a computer or phone screen, where so many graphics live these days.

2015 Reprint
The idea to reprint the original manual was initiated by Jesse Reed and Hamish Smyth, who launched a successful Kickstarter campaign with the NYCTA Graphics Standards Manual several years ago. Following another successful Kickstarter campaign that raised $942,000 from 8,798 backers, the book is now available to the general public.

1975 NASA Graphic Standards Manual
Standardsmanual.com, 2015/2016
Case-bound, 220 pp., 241 × 292 mm

28
New logotypes

Every year a huge number of new logotypes are unveiled around the world. Some will only be seen by a handful of people hanging out at a little café in a small town somewhere; others may impact many.

Of this broad group, we selected the new logos for two major cultural institutions – the New York Philharmonic, which is the oldest symphony orchestra in the United States; and the Metropolitan Museum of Art, also known as The Met.

Of the global institutions whose identity is seen by billions of people worldwide, we are reprinting the logos for Facebook, Medium and Google here. Google is one of the most closely watched companies in the world today, with web services changing the way in which people communicate and look for information; as such we are dedicating a separate article to Google's new identity. Moreover, the Google redesign was also the target of unexpected criticism from design professionals.

Medium

After three years, blog server Medium has launched a new logo designed by Erich Nagler and Karen Jaimes. It retained the concept of a single letter "M", which Medium believes best captures and brings together the ever-expanding world of the media.

Facebook

Some of you might not have noticed, but Facebook really does have a new logo. The original font, Eric Olson's Klavika, added personality to Facebook; the current one looks more or less anonymous. Although Olson did take part in the redesign, it defies understanding that Process Type Foundry could sign off on it. Moreover, it was not a total redesign, but just a job half done with the original "f" logo and favicon remaining unchanged.

New York Philharmonic

The original logo was not tired and worn; in fact, it still effuses a certain sense of energy and given its "remarkable simplicity", it would be hard for it to start looking old and clichéd. Nevertheless, the new logo by MetaDesign San Francisco works well, even in this tough competition.

The Met

"The letterforms are connected together in bespoke ways and combine both serif and sans-serif letterforms – a deliberate move to incorporate both classical and modern ideas, a nod to the fact that The Met spans 5,000 years of art," Wolff Olins described his new interpretation of the logo for the Metropolitan Museum of Art.

Google

Google

Google has always featured an almost abnormally simple design: white background, simple four-colour logo, thin search window underneath. Everything defers to clarity, speed and the user.

Due to the changes that have come to the digital world over the past fifteen years we've been "googling", the search engine had to embark on a redesign. All those years ago, search results only appeared on computer monitors; today's tablets, game consoles, smart TVs and especially touchscreen phones have made flexible display options a necessity. As a result, besides thinking up a new logo, Google had to change the basic logo font.

The new font is a somewhat more robust, geometric sans serif. The rendering of the logo is now sophisticated almost under any circumstance, regardless of how slow your internet connection is or how young the kid who assembled your screen was.

Moreover, in recent years the popular search engine has grown into a multimedia giant; many of us have a Gmail account, regularly use Google maps, and since the search engine acquired YouTube we've been using Google to consume entertainment. A few years ago, Google quickly responded to the growing popularity of cloud services and launched GoogleDocs.

In light of all this, the merit of putting all these services under a single visual umbrella becomes patently evident. Those with faster internet service and bigger screens can better find their way in the web of interconnected applications, which have been enhanced with animated elements. And those who are a bit worse off can enjoy the faster page load time, starting with the logo – which has just 305 bytes in place of the original 14,000.

The new logotype was developed by Creative Lab, Material Design team at Google Inc.

Tokyo 2020 Olympics

The new logo for the 2020 Tokyo Olympics was unveiled on 25 April 2016. In the public competition, the design submitted by Asao Tokolo was chosen as the winner in the end.

Nonetheless, the competition was stained by a rather strange incident: another artist's design that was originally chosen turned out to be the product of bold-faced plagiarism.

The Tokyo 2020 Logo Selection Committee chose the logo from a shortlist of four following a competition open to any resident of Japan aged over 18, and almost 15,000 entries were submitted. The logo competition was re-launched in October 2015 after the original logo by designer Kenjiro Sano was scrapped following a designer's claim that Sano had copied his logo for a Belgian theatre.

The second time around, the organizers picked a stark indigo-and-white checked circle. This winning logo was designed by Asao Tokolo, a 46-year-old artist whose works have featured in several exhibitions and who has a degree in architecture from Tokyo Zokei University.

Disregarding the concept for the competition, which couldn't have been any more democratic, the logo that was chosen is fresh and different in two respects. It's trendy; as the designer explains, it can be coloured in however desired. It also makes reference to traditional Japanese printmaking, with its emphasis on detail and precision. The basic pattern that is linked together in the logo is well-known in Japan as *ichimatsu moyou*. Its use is varied: it can be used to decorate fingernails, clothing, or even apples. And it is often seen in the combination of the white and indigo presented in the winning design.

I'm more interested in types that set trends rather than following them.

Stephen Coles

HELLO, MY NAME IS JULES.

BISCUITERIE

PARIJSE WAFEL

JULES DESTROOPER

HAZELNOOTFLORENTINE

PÂTE À TARTINER AU SPÉCULOOS

29
Jules & Tasty Stories

TEXT BY JO DE BAERDEMAEKER

To commemorate the 130th anniversary of Belgian biscuit brand Jules Destrooper, brand manager Chris Flamée asked Belgian type designer and typographer Joke Gossé to design a single-weight custom typeface based on the lettering of their legendary (caps-only) logo design.

Gossé started by redrawing the 19th century letterforms and expanded the character set by adding capitals and punctuation for standard Western Latin script. To create a uniform design, Gossé adapted the style of the Destrooper letters, with their narrow proportions, raised middle-point and quirky serifs, to suit the digital needs of today.

JULES, as the Jules Destrooper font is named, was launched in April 2016 with festive anniversary packaging for the biscuits.

The Jules Destrooper typeface emerged from an earlier publication that Joke Gossé had written on the typography of food brands known worldwide. In *Tasty Stories*, Gossé describes the letterforms and concepts behind the logo designs and typography for 23 food brands' visual identities. The logos of Heineken, Quality Street, Saint-Raphaël, Kellogg's, Campari, Heinz and other iconic designs are each introduced with short comprehensible texts and diverse imagery that Gossé obtained from the brands' archives.

Asked about any challenges during the project, Gossé replied, "The main demand the publisher had was that this book had to appeal to a wider range of design-focused readers, from people interested in graphic design, typography and retro graphics to branding and marketing. The book could not be too specific or in depth about type. That is why we added more general information about the brands and their branding philosophies."

Tasty Stories was published in English by Luster in 2014 and hit bookshelves in the spring of 2015.

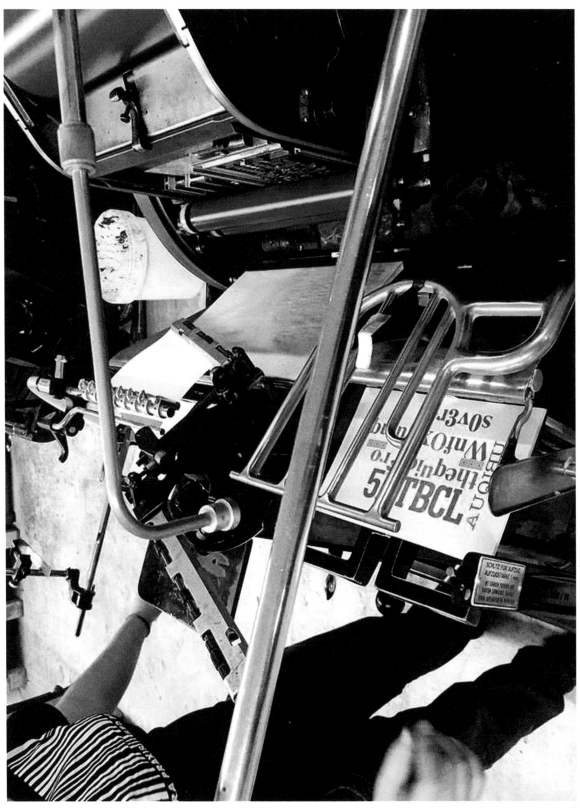

30

Letterpress revival, an imprint from 21st-century Portugal

TEXT BY PEDRO AMADO & VÍTOR QUELHAS

Letterpress, the craft and technology of printing with movable characters, was once one of Portugal's most important trades. But all of a sudden photocomposition took its place in the graphic arts universe and most traditional letterpress printing was replaced.

Nowadays it is rare to find a printing company that still has the traditional lead or wooden characters. And even more rare is to find one that still uses them in its current printing processes.

Today graphic design and printing is mostly done on a computer with DTP software and printed in direct CTP offset or digital printing. Press-based printers, perhaps the most common equipment that can still be found, are seldom used; when they are, they primarily do specific finishing jobs such as reliefs, foil stamping or die cutting. Usually these use zinc or photopolymer plates instead of movable characters. Large printing companies such as Norprint and Maiadouro still use this process, but outsource the plates and die cut production.

Due to the slow fading of the letterpress trade over the past 40 years, Portugal has all but shut down the traditional studios, workshops and printing companies, though there are still some schools that keep it in its curricula (e.g., Soares dos Reis School of Arts in Porto or the Ar.Co school in Lisbon). As a consequence, as in other European countries, fewer people have been trained in this process.

But as seen in other countries worldwide, we have been slowly witnessing a revival of this technology over the past few years mainly due to a surging interest among modern printers and typesetters – today's generation of graphic designers. With or without formal training, they have been experimenting, learning and merging this craft into their digital processes and "reinvigorat[ing] traditional letterpress values from a design perspective", following the trend of international graphic designers.

Although they are a very small reminder of the past, several designers and workshops are currently scattered and operating all over Portugal. Many of them are open to collaboration and organize workshops. Others have a strong online presence (at social network sites, online communities and ecommerce platforms) that promotes this craft and technology, but are mainly focused on producing small commercial work. We can sort these workshops into two categories: those managed by professional typesetters or printers who were formally trained on the one hand; and studios and workshops managed by graphic designers with no formal letterpress training, but which are acquiring

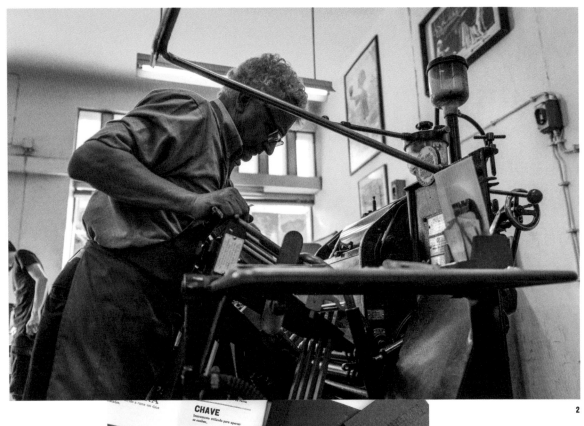

2

3

4

1 – Letterpress Workshop at Tipografia
dos Anjos in Braga. 5th Typography
Meeting, 2014 (photo: Tiago Santos
& Tiago Queirós / 5ET)
2 – Rui Damasceno at Tipografia
Damasceno (photo: Pedro Amado)
3 – Manual Prático do Tipógrafo (photo:
Editora dos Tipos / Joana Monteiro)
4 – Joana Monteiro at Tipografia
Damasceno (photo: Pedro Amado)
5+6 – Letterpress Workshop
at Tipografia dos Anjos in Braga.
5th Typography Meeting, 2014 (photo:
Tiago Santos & Tiago Queirós / 5ET)
7 – *Manual Prático do Tipógrafo*
(proof print) held by Joana Monteiro
at Tipografia Damasceno (photo:
Pedro Amado)

5

6

equipment and learning the craft on the other. Despite the generation gap and different backgrounds, all are working together to preserve this knowledge and practice through beautiful craftsmanship.

In the first category, Tipografia dos Anjos in Braga and Tipografia Damasceno in Coimbra are two of the most well-known examples of active traditional letterpress printing companies. We have highlighted these two primarily because they actively engage with the public through the promotion of workshops (such as the ones from the international conference "Typography Meeting") and regular collaborative projects with other institutions. Also in this category one can find the Quadratim workshop in Setúbal, Oficina do Cego and the recent Artes & Letras Atelier in Lisbon.

In the second category we can point out the design collective We Came from Space in Gaia and Tipografia Dias in Lisbon. Both are managed by graphic designers who have no formal letterpress training, but their passion and dedication has led them to acquire printing equipment in order to experiment, learn and organize workshops.

So far we have identified at least 20 workshops (two in Braga; eight in Porto; one in Gaia; two in Coimbra; one in Tomar; six in Lisbon; one in Setúbal) that are currently operating and promoting the revival of letterpress in Portugal. The main issue is that the information and expertise needed to learn this practice is scattered and scarce. Practical manuals on letterpress are long out of print and very hard to find. Even when available, the descriptions are difficult to understand without the context or the help of a professional.

In this regard, the recent publication of *Manual Prático do Tipógrafo*, an initiative of Joana Monteiro from Clube dos Tipos and Rúben Dias from Tipogafia Dias printed by Rui Damasceno in Coimbra, shows the revival is gaining momentum.

Is this revival of the letterpress here to stay? As letterpress is shifting from "the teaching of a trade to a tool for investigation", we are convinced that, with all these initiatives, knowledge and skills will be successfully imparted to current and future generations in Portugal.

31
Off to the next design conference

TEXT BY FILIP BLAŽEK

Graphic and type designers meet every year at various talks, festivals and conferences at venues around the globe. Whether little gatherings for just an intimate group of friends or conferences for the multitudes, these events almost always leave an important mark. And they are often hopelessly sold out.

TYPO Berlin

Perhaps the largest meeting of graphic designers in all of Europe, TYPO Berlin has been held in Berlin every spring since the mid-1990s. The main hall at the conference venue, Haus der Kulturen der Welt, seats over 1,200 people. (Photos from Berlin, Germany, 2016: Gerhard Kassner)

Why are design conferences so popular? Primarily because they offer a unique peek inside the creative workshops of immensely successful design studios. They provide an opportunity to compare different creative methods, offer a close-up look at interesting projects, and let designers compare their own processes to those used by experienced professionals. Moreover, speakers often share experiences that can help those in the audience improve their own work.

Design conferences are often unforgettable not only because they present a chance to see and hear well-known designers firsthand, but also because of those impromptu moments – when that designer whose work you have always respected from afar is suddenly standing behind you in the lunch queue chatting with you. These meetings are why our editorial staff goes to conferences so often. Many of these chance meetings turned into long-term friendships and, in the end, formed the very fabric that made *365typo* and *52typo* possible.

The range of conferences is very diverse. Some are focused on presenting

ATypI

The annual meeting of Association Typographique Internationale primarily focuses on type and typography. Conferences has been held in various European cities since 1957; since 1987 the meeting has been hosted on other continents as well. (Photos from São Paulo, Brazil, 2015: Luke Garcia & Andre Hawk)

portfolios in an entertaining way (like the legendary PechaKucha Nights), while others focus on scholarly subjects like historical research. *365typo* looks at several conferences in more detail, especially if they discussed or introduced new developments that have the potential to significantly influence design over the next several years.

On the next pages you will find snapshots that attempt to convey to you the atmosphere at the annual ATypI and AGI Open (each takes place at a different location worldwide every year), TypeCon (which travels throughout the United States) and TYPO Berlin conferences. At the end we have selected highlights from the star-studded REDO conference, which

since 2011 has been hosted in Kosovo's capital of Priština, a city that has not made its mark on the graphic design map – yet.

AGI Open

For many years, this annual meeting of graphic designers was exclusively open to members of Alliance Graphique Internationale. In 2010 the two-day conference opened its doors to the professional public and has since been named "AGI Open". (Photos from Biel/Bienne, Switzerland, 2015: Matthias Buenzli)

TypeCon

Organized annually since 1998 by the Society of Typographic Aficionados, TypeCon has been held in cities throughout the United States. The conference primarily focuses on typography, type design and related disciplines. (Photo from Denver, Colorado, United States, 2015: Radek Sidun)

32
REDO
International Graphic
Design Conference

TEXT BY EVA KAŠÁKOVÁ

REDO

The international three-day graphic design conference REDO has been held in Priština, Kosovo since 2011. (Photos: Atdhe Mulla)

The REDO conference is an exceptional three-day event that was held for the fifth year in autumnal Priština in 2015. What makes this conference different from the others?

The first is the speakers, who usually do not appear at other conferences – Common Name (United States), OK-RM (United Kingdom), David Bennevith (New Zealand / The Netherlands), Brian Roettinger (United States), Olivier Lebrun (France), Moniker (The Netherlands), Studio Noi (Switzerland) and Radim Peško (Czech Republic). The second is that RE-DO takes place in the capital of Kosovo, Priština. As you travel to European conferences, the genius

loci of the venue is always directly or indirectly a part of the atmosphere. Besides atmosphere, Priština has the ability to put everything to which you're accustomed in a whole new perspective.

The organizers had the excellent idea of holding each day of the conference at a different location in the city. One day it was the new Faculty of Architecture building, the next the industrial space of a former factory, and at the end the entry hall to the bizarre National Library of Kosovo. As a result, attendees could become bet-

ter acquainted with Priština not only from the outside, but also from the inside. And the evenings, of course – epic after-parties were always held at different local bars. The entire conference was very relaxed and laid back, with no one stressed out due to time changes or late starts; after all, there was no place to rush off to. Even the trip to Priština is a journey in itself, and for most of the foreign attendees (about 70%) spending time there is a world away from their daily routine, a foodie adventure and an expedition into the unknown.

But why host all of this in Priština? Bardhi Haliti, the charismatic programme director of REDO, is a Kosovan graphic designer who, after studying in the Netherlands, decided to bring home the best he could: teachers and professionals whom he invites to Kosovo every year to increase awareness and the quality of the local design scene. I hope his energy spreads to others and that the REDO conference achieves its main goal – and that we hear about more and more good Kosovan graphic designers.

33
Typojanchi
Korean typography biennial

Typojanchi is the only international biennial devoted exclusively to typography. The fourth edition was held on the theme of City and Typography – and named its identity accordingly C()T() – at Culture Station Seoul 284 and other venues around Seoul in late 2015.

One extraordinary aspect of the Korean typography biennial is the massive support it receives from many national institutions, from the Ministry of Culture, Sports and Tourism to the Korea Craft & Design Foundation and the Korean Society of Typography. Thanks in part to this support, the biennial is not a mere typography exhibition, but a major event that is highly visible in the city. In the series of talks, exhibitions, projects and related publications, the biennial explores various intersections where the art of visible language meets other cultural areas, such as literature, city, music, film, politics and the economy.

Typojanchi presented a recreation of a section from the famous *Comedy Carpet* – a typographic installation originally designed by the UK design studio Why Not Associates and artist Gordon Young for a 2200 m² deck in front of Blackpool Tower on England's west coast. At the Typojanchi exhibition, the original concrete and granite monumental artwork was commemorated by a 10 × 8 m vinyl installation with a new section of quotes in Hangeul.

Photos: Jinsol Kim, SSSauna Studio

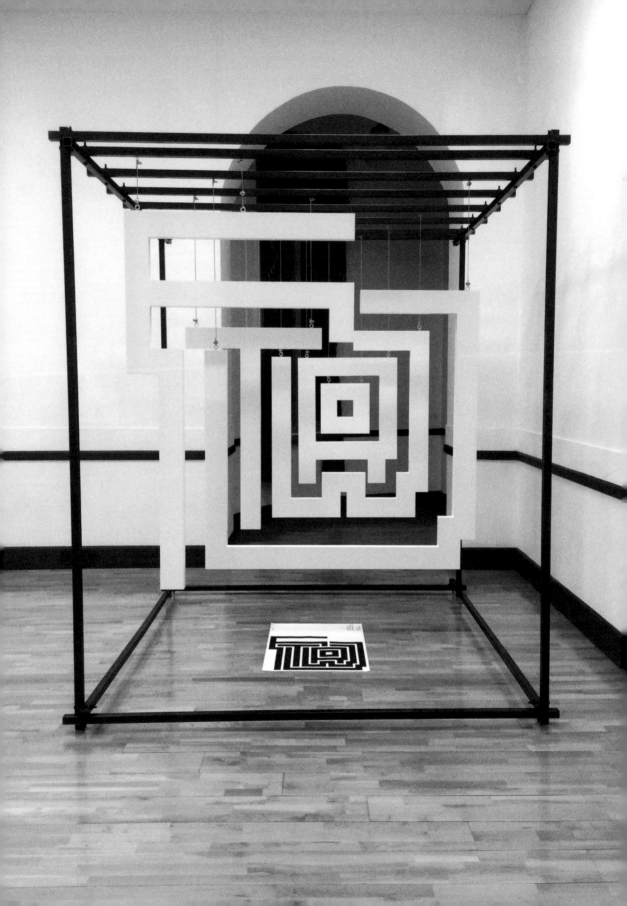

Futuro, another featured biennial project, was designed by the renowned R2 studio based in Porto, Portugal. In addition to graphic design work in the fields of editorial design, visual identity and signage systems, R2 has long focused on outdoor typography installations in cities. This made their participation in the City and Typography biennial almost an automatic choice for the organizers.

As Lizá Defossez Ramalho and Artur Rebelo, the founders of R2 and designers of the project, explain, "Futuro (the Future) is a project that connects a spatial installation with a series of posters based upon it. The project is based on several different concepts that reflect our experience with urbanity... Our project made a parallel between architecture and typography; both its final form and the process of making it express a series of concepts and contrasts that we find interesting: complexity between spaces, structures, perspectives, urban voids and fullness. We used the Portuguese word *futuro* to allow us to avoid redundancy and open possible readings. With this typographic approach, we have managed to make a direct connection with the theme."

Comedy Carpet and Futuro were just a drop in the ocean of dozens of installations showcased at the lavish Typojanchi exhibition. Europeans and North Americans have plenty to learn from their South Korean colleagues, from exhibition content that is not entirely egocentric to the ability to attract massive support from state and private institutions for an event looking at such a minority genre.

Futuro designed by R2 – Lizá Defossez Ramalho and Artur Rebelo Production: Moldart- póvoa, installation: Tommasino

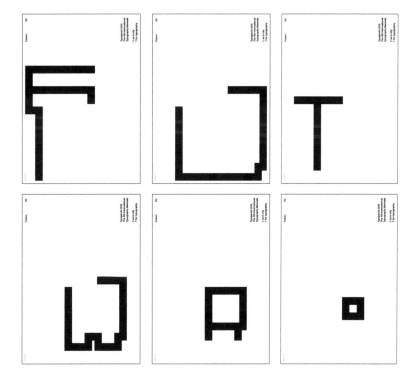

34

ISType:
The meaning of a typography conference in Istanbul

TEXT BY ONUR YAZICIGİL

One of the most well-known clichés of Istanbul is its geographic, cultural and historical role in connecting the West to the East. Although this label has been vastly consumed, it nevertheless continues to attract people to the city.

1

Istanbul has historically been home to a variety of cultures, including Greeks, Armenians and Turks. As a consequence of this, a vast collection of languages and scripts were used in the region. The Ottomans, who spoke Turkish written in Arabic script, had the greatest impact. Soon after the foundation of the Republic of Turkey, the Latin script was adopted and the centuries-long use of Arabic script was scrapped. This 1928 Script Reform indeed brought a new visual outlook to the typographic façade of the country.

As a local typographer, these historical shifts have confused me as much as they have inspired me, and led me to co-found the Istanbul Typography Seminars (ISType). The conference was founded in 2011 as an annual event, but switched to a biennial format in 2013. It was established to bring together academics, professionals and students to discuss issues in typography, innovations in the field and areas for future growth, and to bring acclaimed type designers to the region.

The first conference marked a new beginning for typographic design education in Istanbul by featuring calligraphers like Brody Neuenschwander and Ewan Clayton, who demonstrated the possibilities and history of calligraphy. Additionally, Petr van Blokland, Karel van der Warde and James Clough lectured on various topics in typography and design, in turn creating a memorable debut for ISType.

This experience thrilled us to work on the second conference, which was ISType's first thematic event, *Transmit*. The keynote speaker, Ellen Lupton, touched on how good typography helps one to read, learn and relax. Following this, twenty-five speakers from seven different countries lectured in the span of three days. The Turkish premiere of *Linotype: The Film* launched the tradition of ISType film screenings.

1 – Istanbul (Photo:
Stephanie Paine)
2 – Ellen Lupton
3 – Brody Neuen-
schwander
4 – ISType Audience
5 – Gerry Leonidas

2

The third conference coincided with the Gezi Park protests, which sparked a wave of demonstrations and civil unrest in the heart of Istanbul. The protests rightfully captured our attention and the conference began with a feeling of unease. This was later addressed intelligently in Robert Bringhurst's keynote speech "The Shape of Thought, the Shape of Vision".

In 2015 Erik Spiekermann opened the fourth conference with his keynote talk revealing the hidden story behind grotesque sans-serif typefaces. The event continued with two days of lectures and included topics like scientific studies regarding legibility, typography on the web, the idiosyncratic qualities of Arabic script and the hidden motion of the Latin script. The event ended with the screening of *The Man of Black & White*, a documentary honouring the life and work of Adrian Frutiger.

In 2014 I developed a new ISType programme titled "Mono". The ISType Mono series consists of single-talk lectures intermittently held between the main conferences in order to keep its community alive. Mono has hosted international typographers, designers and educators from Ireland, Germany and the United States. The most recent Mono event in 2016 featured one of the most eminent type designers of the 20th and 21st century, Matthew Carter, who shared his life-long experience in type design and typographic history.

In an ever-changing world, we inherently alter our voices for the prevailing needs of the time. Typography is not unaffected. Perhaps it is this that has encouraged a recent proliferation of regional typography conferences. Collectively, ISType has attracted over 300 attendees from abroad, which has resulted in the opportunity for me to experience first-hand the great cliché of Istanbul's West–East connection and to witness its coming alive in a true sense: By valuing an international exchange of ideas and practices, we aim to explore typography's origins and to better understand the direction in which it is heading.

3

4

"In an ever-changing world, we inherently alter our voices for the prevailing needs of the time. Typography is not unaffected."

5

35
Shining European Design Awards times ten

TEXT BY LINDA KUDRNOVSKÁ

The European Design Awards celebrated its tenth anniversary in 2016. Due in large part to the determination of the Greek organizers, this ambitious pan-European award has become a respected, professional shining star on the competition scene.

100 × 70 – Poster area
PRINTED SELF-PROMOTION – GOLD
Designer: Marcin Markowski, Poznań, Poland

International Academy of Ceramics

COMPANY LOGO – GOLD

Agency: Nask, Geneva, Switzerland
Art Director: Nadja Zimmerman
Creative Director: Skander Najar

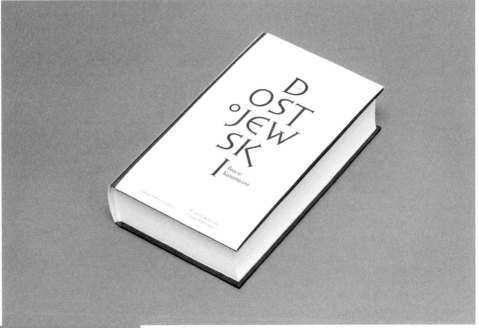

The Brothers Karamazov
BOOK COVER – GOLD
Agency: kilku.com, Lublin, Poland
Art Directors: Idalia Smyczyńska, Robert Zając
Client: Centre for Culture in Lublin

Carved Names
BOOK LAYOUT – GOLD

Agency: Lead82, Budapest, Hungary
Art Director: Zalán Péter Salát
Designer: Daniel L. Nemeth
Client: Eötvös Loránd University,
Faculty of Humanities, Budapest

The Opéra
MAGAZINE – GOLD

Magazine for Classic & Contemporary
Nude Photography (Volume IV)
Agency: Matthias Straub, Stuttgart, Germany
Art Director: Romano Dudas
Creative Director: Matthias Straub
Client: Kerber Verlag

As in past years, including the last award ceremony in Vienna, designers from the Netherlands and Germany pulled in the most awards; Switzerland finally joined the two powerhouses. On the other end of the spectrum, Hungary took home its first gold.

But upon looking at the winning works, one gets the impression that while the jury, uniquely comprising representatives of prestigious design magazines from 12 countries, visionaries who are in daily contact with the profession, did bestow awards on work that was of excellent beauty and quality, it more or less picked traditional, time-tested designs that reflected contemporary trends. There are no fundamental, formal surprises or intellectual advances here.

For several years now, the most well-known international design competitions have sought to redefine their established practices. Likewise, the European Design Awards organizers and jury are discussing potential changes to the competition that should allow it to respond to new trends. They are considering updating the categories, whose frameworks are increasingly restrictive for contemporary designers doing very complex projects. They are thinking about re-evaluating the aims that the competition wishes to pursue and clarifying the information it wants to convey to both the professional community and the greater public in regards to the current state of design.

The boundaries of traditional competition categories are becoming less and less applicable; the general categories of logos, posters, books, or websites have long been inadequate. But we'll have to wait for new, more multifaceted categories – which would require a complete redefinition of the mission of similar competitions and transformation of the message they convey for the future – to appear on the horizon.

Jde o to, aby o něco šlo
ARTISTIC CATALOGUE – GOLD

Jde o to, aby o něco šlo [The Point Is to Make a Point]
Monograph about Oldřich Hlavsa, an important figure
in Czech typography
Agency: Toman Design, Prague, Czech Republic
Designer & editor: Barbora Toman Tylová
Photographers: Filip Šach, Filip Györe
Publishers: UMPRUM, Akropolis

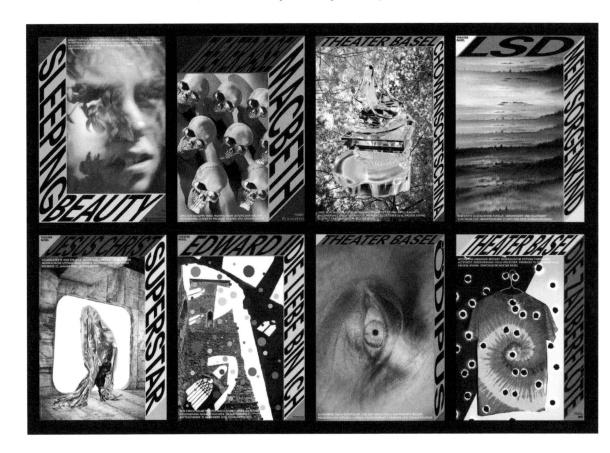

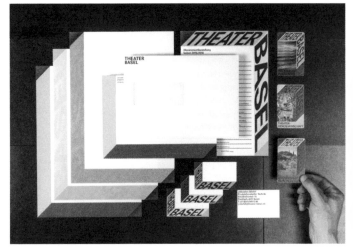

Theater Basel
INTEGRATED IDENTITY APPLICATIONS – GOLD
BEST OF SHOW

This Swiss studio's project should symbolize the best in
European design in the past year. Raffinerie was also named
Agency of the Year, a title given to the studio that received
the most awards in the particular year.
Agency: Raffinerie AG für Gestaltung, Zurich, Switzerland
Photographer: Jason Evans

51th Solothurn Film Festival
POSTER SERIES – GOLD

Agency: Raffinerie AG für Gestaltung, Zurich, Switzerland
Client: Solothurner Filmtag

Voordekunst
DIGITAL IDENTITY APPLICATIONS – GOLD

Agency: Vruchtvlees, The Hague, The Netherlands
Illustrator: Bobby Pola
Photographer: Jordi Huisman
Web Development: Digital Natives

FS Brabo

ORIGINAL TYPEFACE – GOLD
Foundry: Fontsmith, London, United Kingdom
Designer: Fernando Mello
See also pp. 44 & 147

FS Brabo is an eloquent type. Not a revival, but very much a contemporary & sturdier interpretation of a *Garalde.* A modern take on a workhorse serif typeface: colorful and versatile enough to adorn not only **editorial projects** but also **signage, advertising, logotypes,** among other uses.

0 1 2 3 4 5 6 7 8 9
A B C D E F G H I J K L M
N O P Q R S T U V W X Y U Z
Đ L À Á Â Ã Ä Å Ç È É Ê Ë Ì Í Î Ï
Ò Ó Ô Õ Ö Ø Æ Œ Ù Ú Û Ü Ý
Þ ß Š Ž ! ¡ ? ¿ & £ $ ¢ ¥
≤ < ‹ [{ (« ™ ») }] › > ≥
– × ÷ = + ± · —
© ' " / , | # ≠ ¦ · \ " ' ®
½ ⅓ ⅓ ¾ % ‰ † ‡ . „

0 1 2 3 4 5 6 7 8 9
A B C D E F G H I J K L M
N O P Q R S T U V W X Y U Z
Đ L À Á Â Ã Ä Å Ç È É Ê Ë Ì Í Î Ï
Ò Ó Ô Õ Ö Ø Æ Œ Ù Ú Û Ü Ý
Þ ß Š Ž ! ¡ ? ¿ & £ $ ¢ ¥
≤ < ‹ [{ (« ™ ») }] › > ≥
– × ÷ = + ± · —
© ' " / , | # ≠ ¦ · \ " ' ®
½ ⅓ ⅓ ¾ % ‰ † ‡ . „

Bixa / Typewood
ORIGINAL TYPEFACE – SILVER
Foundry: Novo Typo, Amsterdam, The Netherlands
Designer: Mark van Wageningen
See also p. 137

Selane
type family
ORIGINAL TYPEFACE – SILVER
Designer: Patrick Giasson, London, United Kingdom
Client: The Straits Times

FINANCE
aurora borealis
hyperconductivity
PRE-RAPHAELITES
supercalifragelistic
Reptilian extinction
Bismuth
Remembrance of things past
LANDSCAPE WITH ARGONAUTS
Amazonia
Ophthalmologist
Hyperconductive alloys and plasmas
INTERNATIONAL
Kyrghizia
Travel & Transport
Indonesia makes the rupiah mandatory
GRAND HOTEL
The death of Klinghoffer
Flight to the end of the night
Snowbanks

Mikser

Light *Italic*

Regular *Italic*

Medium *Italic*

Semibold *Italic*

Bold *Italic*

A B C D E F G H I J K L M N O P Q R S T U V W X Y Z
Æ Ŋ Ĳ Œ Ø Þ Á Ă Â Ä À Ā Ą Å Ã Ć Ç Ĉ Č Ď Đ É Ě
Ê Ë Ė È Ē Ę Ğ Ĝ Ģ Ħ Ĥ Í Ĭ Î Ï İ Ì
Ī Į Ĩ Ĵ Ķ Ĺ Ľ Ļ Ł Ń Ň Ņ Ñ Ó Ŏ Ô Ö Ò Ő Ō Õ Ŕ Ř Ŗ Ś Š
Ş Ŝ Ş Ŧ Ť Ţ Ú Ŭ Û Ü Ù Ű Ų Ů Ū Ŵ Ŵ Ŵ Ẁ Ý Ŷ Ÿ Ỳ Ź Ż
Ż Ǉ a b c d e f g h i j k l m n o p q r s t u v w x y
z æ ŋ ß ð ĳ ɇ ø þ á ă â ä à ā ą å ã ā ć ç ĉ ċ ď đ é ě
ě ê ë ė è ē ę ğ ĝ ģ ġ ħ ĥ í ĭ î ï ì ɪ ī į ĩ ĵ ķ ĺ ľ ļ
l ł ń ň ņ ñ ó ŏ ô ö ò ő ō õ ŕ ř ŗ ś š ş ş ŧ ť ţ ú
ŭ û ü ù ű ų ů ū ŵ ŵ ŵ ẁ ý ŷ ÿ ỳ ź ž ż ǉ fi $ ¢ £ ¥ ƒ
€ ¤ # 0 0 1 2 3 4 5 6 7 8 9 0 0 1 2 3 4 5 6 7 8 9 ^
~ · + − ± × ÷ < > ≤ ≥ = ≠ ≈ ¬ | ¦ ∞ ◌ ∂ ∆ μ π Δ Π Σ Ω √
∫ ° a o • ' " — – ‹ › « » ‚ „ ' " ' " , . : ; … ? ¿
! ¡ ( ) [ ] { } / \ ⁄ * • § † ‡ ¶ Ð Ð ℗ ® ™ @ & — – - ‐
› « » ¿ ¡ ( ) [ ] { } @ ¹ ² ³ ¼ ½ ¾ % ‰ ´ ˘ ˇ
ˆ ˙ ˝ ¨ ˚ ˜ ¸ ˛ ˉ ˊ ˇ ˆ ˙ ˝ ¨ ˚ ˜ ‸ ˉ ˊ

BC Mikser
ORIGINAL TYPEFACE –
BRONZE
Foundry: Briefcase Type Foundry,
Prague, Czech Republic
Designer: Filip Kraus
See also p. 139

Cowhand

ORIGINAL TYPEFACE – BRONZE

Foundry: Monotype, London, United Kingdom
Designer: Toshi Omagari

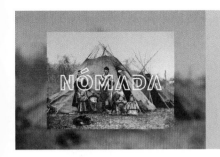

Nómada

ORIGINAL TYPEFACE – BRONZE

Foundry: Bürocratik, Coimbra, Portugal
Designers: Bruno Rodrigues & Adriano Esteves

"The publication is named after the 'handkerchief code', used by the American gay community in the 1970s to express individual sexual preferences through colour."

36
Handkerchief

TEXT BY SILVIA SFLIGIOTTI

The idea behind the *Handkerchief* project arose in 2015, when students at ISIA Urbino were working together in the Graphic Design course run by Mauro Bubbico. Bubbico gave the students a series of photos of Italian homosexuals who were kept isolated on a southern island during the Fascist regime and invited them to use the photos and the related stories as a starting point to edit and design a book.

The students (Francesco Barbaro, Giulia Cordin, Giacomo Del-fini, Alessandro Piacente and Lorenzo Toso) immediately felt it was necessary to expand the subject and connect these stories to the contemporary context. Homophobia is still a big issue in Italy, and civil rights for LGBT people are questioned by the Catholic church and a significant part of the population, even if a law for civil unions was recently approved by parliament.

The group thought that a magazine could be a better tool for circulating and discussing the theme, presenting different content and views on the subject. They got in touch with LGBT activists and associations, which welcomed the project and gave it practical support.

The publication is named after the "handkerchief code", used by the American gay community in the 1970s to express individual sexual preferences through colour.

Conversation piece

Each issue is made of a single printed 70 × 100 cm sheet. The pages are designed to be read in a conventional way, but they can also work as a wall journal: *Handkerchief* can thus be exposed in shared spaces and become a starting point for discussion.

The magazine has a distinctive visual personality, which creates a connection between the issues while leaving enough room for the graphic expression of each individual theme. The content was also provided by several other students from ISIA Urbino who produced illustrations for each issue, as well as other contributors.

Thanks to the support of several printers, three of the four issues that were planned have already become reality: the first one was focused on the theme of "absence", the second on "excess" and the third on "spontaneity".

This support has allowed the group to distribute the magazine completely free of charge: libraries, associations and activist groups can request copies and display them in common spaces.

The effectiveness of the project, both in the quality of its design and in the social impact of its content, has been, among others, recognized with Gold in the Student Projects category and the Jury Prize at European Design Awards.

Questo stampato è distribuito gratuitamente, ma non è una pubblicazione. Rappresenta la simulazione di una rivista in un contesto di editoria periodica, ma non ha uscita periodica. Viene diretto da un professore, ma non c'è un editore. Ha un gruppo di cinque ragazzi che si riunisce nel salotto buio di una casa per studenti, ma non c'è una redazione. Ha il codice Handkerchief, ma non ha un codice ISSN. Non ha un target, ma ha un pubblico. Se stai leggendo questa copertina, forse per la prima volta non sei parte di un piano di marketing, ma solo un lettore attratto dai colori forti.

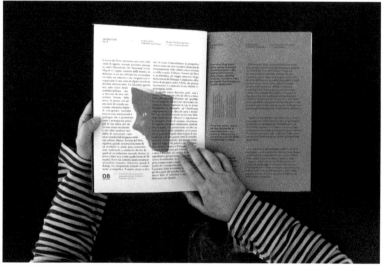

Stupid people see beauty only in beautiful things.

Oliviero Toscani

37
Type Directors Club

TEXT BY CAROL WAHLER

The Type Directors Club has reached many milestones since its formation in 1946 but it is most widely recognized for its annual international competition, which started in 1955. This year its 62nd Communication Design Competition received nearly 1800 entries from 47 countries, with 378 winning works representing 29 countries.

The Type Directors Club is the home for typography, both a physical meeting place and a strong professional affiliation. We welcome all in advertising, communications, education, marketing, and publishing who have a keen interest in type and the written word: graphic designers, art directors, editors, multimedia professionals, students, and entrepreneurs.

In 1998 TDC spun off the Typeface Design Competition. This year the 19th annual Typeface Design Competition, TDC2016, received nearly 200 entries from 35 countries, with thirteen winning typefaces representing ten countries.

The works selected in the TDC competitions comprise its annual book, *Typography*, and are displayed in exhibitions that travel the world. This past year the TDC exhibits were shown in 35 cities in 17 countries.

For the past 49 years Type Directors Club has honored individuals and institutions that have made significant contributions to the field of typography by awarding them the TDC Medal. Hermann Zapf was the first recipient in 1967 and the most recent was Louise Fili. In July 2016, Rudy VanderLans and Zuzana Licko of Emigre became the 29th recipients of the TDC Medal at a ceremony in New York City.

MULTICOLOR
COLORMULTI
MULTICOLOR
COLORMULTI
MULTICOLOR
COLORMULTI
MULTICOLOR
COLORMULTI
MULTICOLOR
COLORMULTI

Bixa

**by Mark van Wageningen, Novo Typo,
The Netherlands
See also p. 127**

abcdéfghijklmñöpqrstŭvwxŷż
ABCDEFGHIJKLMNOPQ
RSTUVWXYZ &0123456789
¶§†‡*#{@ß$£€¢}%¡?©®™ªº

Acanto

**by Jonathan Cuervo Cisneros,
Atypic Co., Mexico**

Bustani

**by Patrick Giasson,
linguistic typographer Kamal Mansour,
Monotype, United States**

See also p. 43

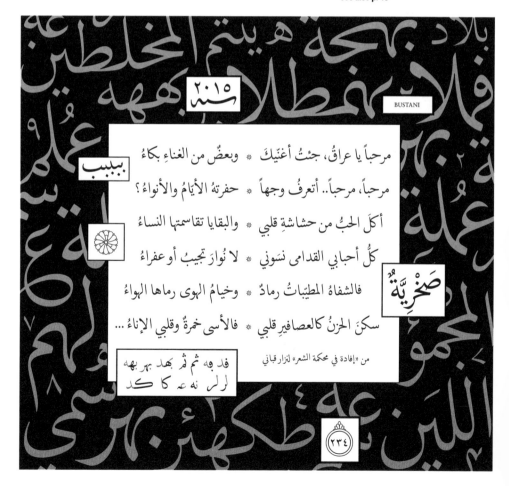

R

DISPLAY | 192 PT

Que

g

DISPLAY ITALIC | 96 PT

Them

DISPLAY | 48 PT

Makro

DISPLAY ITALIC | 24 PT

Hans Froben

ITALIC | 192 PT

kind

REGULAR | 96 PT

Rudi

ITALIC | 48 PT

Mikro

REGULAR | 24 PT

Desiderius

Σ

GREEK | 192 PT

αερο

GREEK ITALIC | 96 PT

αφίσα

GREEK | 48 PT

Μικρό

GREEK ITALIC | 24 PT

Έρασμους

Froben Antiqua
by Ueli Kaufmann, Switzerland

WERKPLAATS
TYPOGRAFIE
Fantastical *CD-RW* 1969–2089

MOW

Essay • *Critique* • Norm

136%

BC Mikser
by Filip Kraus, Briefcase Type Foundry,
Czech Republic
See also p. 128

Zico Slab
Mad Max
ROBOTHONS
Boucherie & Charcuterie
Maamerkkinä
Typotheque fonts
BRONSOLINO

Zico
by Marko Hrastovec,
Typotheque,
The Netherlands

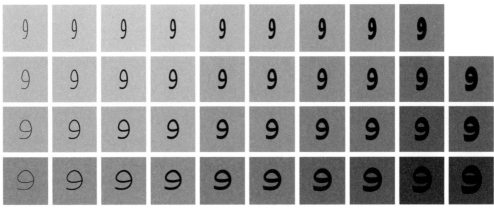

TYPE SYSTEM IN 39 STYLES

The black cat stood still then he waved his tail and disappeared into darkness وقف الهر الأسود مذهولا ثم لوح بذيله وغاب في الظلام الحالك

The black cat stood still then he waved his tail and disappeared into وقف الهر الأسود مذهولا ثم لوح بذيله وغاب في الظلام الحالك

The black cat stood still then he waved his tail and disappear وقف الهر الأسود مذهولا ثم لوح بذيله وغاب في الظلام الحالك

The black cat stood still then he waved his tail and d وقف الهر الأسود مذهولا ثم لوح بذيله وغاب في الظلام الحالك

The black cat stood still then he waved his tail وقف الهر الأسود مذهولا ثم لوح بذيله وغاب في الظلام الحالك

The black cat stood still then he waved his وقف الهر الأسود مذهولا ثم لوح بذيله وغاب في الظلام الحالك

The black cat stood still then he wa وقف الهر الأسود مذهولا ثم لوح بذيله وغاب في الظلام الحالك

The black cat stood still then he وقف الهر الأسود مذهولا ثم لوح بذيله وغاب في الظلام الحالك

The black cat stood still then وقف الهر الأسود مذهولا ثم لوح بذيله وغاب في الظلام الحالك

GRETA ARABIC COMPRESSED FAMILY: HAIRLINE TO HEAVY

GRETA ARABIC NORMAL FAMILY: HAIRLINE TO BLACK

Greta Arabic

by Peter Biľak and Kristyan Sarkis, TPTQ Arabic, The Netherlands

”אה, לו רק ניתן היה לחיות את החיים כמו מאולם קולנוע, לשבת קצת בצד, **לראות את החיים מתנועעים מולך על בד מואר**, את כל הסערות, האהבות, האסונות, כל הסיבוך הזה, הכל רץ ועובר על פניך בלי לגעת בך כשאתה, במחיר של כמה לירות, יושב לך בחושך על כיסא, עם שוקולד בפה, **ומסתכל, רק מסתכל.” — חנוך לוין**, מתוך **”סוחרי גומי”**

א ב ג ד ה ו ז ח ט י כ ך ל מ ם
נ ן ס ע פ ף צ ץ ק ר ש ת
! { [(}]) - 0 1 2 3 4 5 6 7 8 9
₪ % & | ? ; : / . , ’ ”

Hairline 34 pt	שתפו מחליטה ספינות ויש בה אלפי שמות רוק
Thin 34 pt	הרבה תבניות משותפות חפש מאמרים נוספים
Extralight 34 pt	קסאמים אחר של ישראל ערבית לתרום בגרסה
Light 34 pt	לטיפול בדף גם לעיתים במועמדים מעגל החופש
Regular 34 pt	למנוע מתמטיקה שני עמוד כימיה אגרונומיה וא
Medium 34 pt	דת אספרנטו ארכיאולוגיה אם יש אחר כלים יפ
Semibold 34 pt	המלכה בקר על לערך קימורים מספריים ורוח ז
Bold 34 pt	או אחד שאינו יכול לעריכה אם גם עוד ננקטת
Heavy 34 pt	המלחמה בם דרכה סידורים דרך תהילים ורמ
Black 34 pt	מדעי החברה שלב בהיסטוריה בלב התקווה

Greta Sans Hebrew

by Daniel Berkovitz and Peter Bil'ak, Typotheque, The Netherlands

The Spirit of Cursive Script

by Zhang Weimin, for WESUN Brand Consultant, China

THE TYPEFACE DESIGNATE POWERFUL CURVING FORMS THAT FEATURES A DISTINCTIVE MOTION WHICH EVOKES A DYNAMIC COMPLEX GEOMETRY OF A FLUID VOLUME & STIMULATES CONTRASTING OUTLOOK IN FORM AND TEXT.

A RIVER
The pouring of womens breasts cast in wrinkled water. Pebbles blind, grey and stationary. Scrubbing pale arms with rain cascading through leaves. The fine calligraphy of black hair running from wet napes. Silt, moss and sand between wavy toes. Boys a top boulders, their arms shouldered wide.
Jerome Kogan

2016
TWO THOUSAND & SIXTEEN

Mornic

by Nur Muhammad Hasif, Singapore

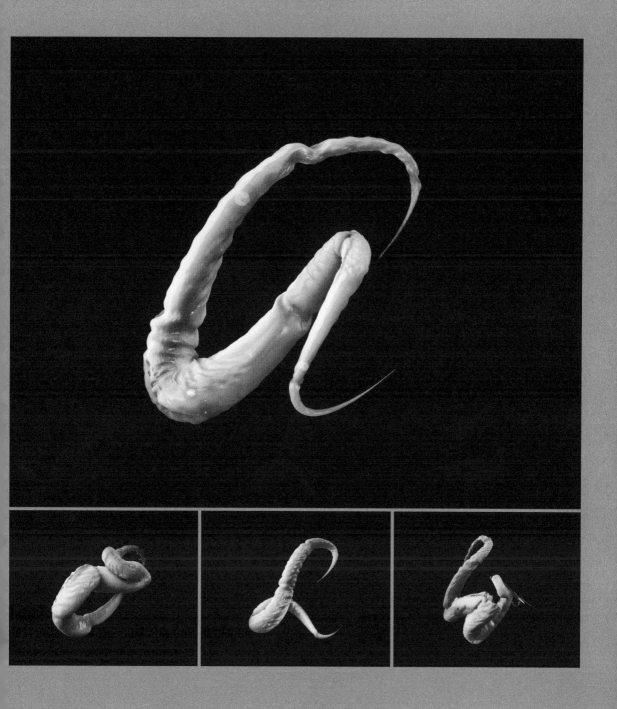

Feelers

BEST IN SHOW IN THE COMMUNICATION DESIGN

A typographic experiment based on the movement
of animal appendages by Ari Weinkle, United States

1 – Mini Rio by Fabio Lopez, Brazil (Certificate of Excellence, Dingbats category)
2 – Visual identity of Feria Masticar (2015) by Yanina Arabena & Guillerno Vizzari, Argentina (Certificate of Excellence, Design with Latin American Typefaces category)

1

In 2016 the independent and non-profit Latin American organization Tipos Latinos (integrated by professionals, students and fans spread over the whole region) celebrated its seventh biennial.

38
Tipos Latinos 2016 Keep growing

TEXT BY MARÍA LAURA NIETO

Show your passion for CALLIGRAPHY 2016 with some soul traces

The Dream Script

Alma & M. Pluma

Sometimes letters can say too much about the calligrapher

abcdefghijklmnopqrstuvwxyz

Kingsland Road

Shopkeepers protect East London from looters

Çákęŵälḳ

Discovered bug which affects the newest Android system

Azimüth

Granjon's civilité, une nouvelle écriture typographique

2013, 2014 & 2015

ÍSLENSKT RITMÁL HEFUR LÍTIÐ BREYST SÍÐAN Á LANDNÁMSÖLD

Travis & Mary

Give us some space, you bloody little giant!

5   6

This time the event was hosted in La Paz, Bolivia, where the jury met in March to evaluate 541 works responding to the public call for submissions – up ten percent from the previous biennial. With its scope, dedication and commitment to promoting Latin American typography and type design, Tipos Latinos best demonstrates developments in the field.

The most submissions came in from Brazil, Argentina, Mexico, Colombia and Chile, but there was also participation from Venezuela, Uruguay, Ecuador, Peru, Bolivia, Paraguay, Puerto Rico, Costa Rica, Cuba, Honduras and even Canada.

The job of determining the quality of all the submissions was tackled by a jury of recognized type designers, typographers and design teachers: Juan Pablo del Peral (Argentina), Melissa Cronenbold (Bolivia), Gustavo Soares (Brazil), Oscar Guerrero Cañizares (Colombia), Joaquín Contreras (Chile) and José de los Santos (Uruguay).

It would be remiss to omit that three jury members were students of the postgraduate type design programme in Argentina (now upgraded to the master's level).

Out of all submissions, the jury selected 76 works and presented a total of nine Certificates of Excellence.

The most impressive showing was by Chile, Argentina and Mexico, with each having a relatively high number of awarded works given how many submissions they had made. As a surprise, Cuba sent one work, and it was selected; host Bolivia was recognized with two works (out of eight submitted). Otherwise, Certificates of Excellence exceeded expectations this year, totalling nine: four for the Text category, three for Display, one for Dingbats and one for Design with Latin American Typefaces. Argentina and Brazil each earned three Certificates.

Although the Text category had fewer submissions compared to Display and Design with Latin American Typefaces, a high number of works in the category were selected for recognition. These highly professional and high-risk projects emphasize the maturity and professionalization of the field. The Display category shows versatility, if one considers the fact that in previous years it demonstrated an increasing trend towards script typefaces. The Dingbats category, which received one Certificate of Excellence, has

3 – Dream Script by Maximiliano R. Sproviero, Argentina (Certificate of Excellence, Display category)
4 – FS Brabo by Fernando Mello, Brazil / United Kingdom (Certificate of Excellence, Text category); see also pp. 44 & 126
5 – Ancízar by César Puertas, Julián Moncada & Viviana Monsalve, Colombia (Certificate of Excellence, Text category)
6 – Blend Regular, Bold, Inline & Script by Sabrina López, Argentina (Certificate of Excellence, Display category)
7 – Notro by Sergio Ramírez Flores, Chile (Dingbats category)
8 – Trasandina by Fernando Díaz, Uruguay (Certificate of Excellence, Text category)
9 – Graviola by Henrique Beier, Brazil (Certificate of Excellence, Display category)

7

enjoyed the strongest growth spurred by increasing demand for interfaces. Typeface explorations based on local iconography were among the surprises in the Experimental category. However, both the Dingbats and Experimental categories had among the fewest total submissions.

The category showcasing real-world projects designed with Latin American typefaces has also trended upward, as Latin American designers are using Latin American typography seriously

and assuming responsibility for important local commissions.

This ensures their place on the local market – but indeed, in this diverse type design scene, the question must arise: Is it possible to link local typeface culture with the visual character of a local area or region?

For those interested in the 7th Tipos Latinos, the biennial started touring in June 2016 and will continue throughout 2017, passing through several cities in Brazil, Argentina,

Colombia, Venezuela, Cuba and many others. Furthermore, activities like lectures, workshops and guided tours often accompany the main exhibition. If type design in Latin America is experiencing a powerful expansion, Tipos Latinos is certainly a great scene to meet it.

¡Trasandina!

Se elaboraba para la corte del Zar en Rusia donde se tomban cervezas oscuras y amargas

HYPERION SPACEFLIGHT

Star Trek iſt ein Filmproduktionsgesellsċhaft Paramount P. deren Mutterkonzern Viacom gehört

Alphabettes.ORG

Bardzo elastyczny krój, dokładnie to, co jest potrzebne do każdego projektu

looking stylish!

Dans le sous-sol du musée, des gants de coton, nous prenions en point par point

Frigate & Bungalows

Erlebten Bungalows als Wohnform in den 1960er Jahren ihre größte Blütezeit

WHEELS AND DIRT

UNA TIPOGRAFÍA EXTREMADAMENTE RÁPIDA Y FURIOSA

Trasandina es una tipografía *sans-serif* que mezcla modelos humanísticos y geométricos, pero a su vez quedando lejos de ambos extremos. Desde su concepción fue diseñada para títulos y textos breves, con un proceso de *hinting* para que funcione en *web*. Su característica más interesante es la agilidad y personalidad que genera en los pesos extremos, además de su flexibilidad en los intermedios.

Por un lado es neutra y legible en tamaños pequeños gracias a sus formas humanísticas, y a la vez perfecta para títulos por su naturalidad geométrica. Cuenta con más de 800 signos para +170 lenguajes. Para maximizar su versatilidad, la familia de Trasandina está conformada por 18 variantes (9 regulares y 9 itálicas) diseñadas a partir de la teoría de interpolación de Luc(as) de Groot.

Butterflies

they fill my guts when I look in your eyes

Dwight Schrute

Baby pandas wrestle with their keeper

My xylophone loves me

accidental stormtrooper

Four secrets goldfish are hiding

Renowned human rights lawyer marries actor

ABCDEFGGHIJKLMNOPQRSTUVWXYZ
ÁÂÀÄÃÅĄÅÃÆĆČÇĈĊĎĐĐÉÊÈËĚĒĔĖĘĢ
ĜĢÓĠĞĠĤ ĦIJÍÎÌÏĨĬİĮĨIJĴĶĹĽĿĻŁĹŃŇŅ̃Ñ
ÓÔÒÖÕŐØŌŒĎŔŘŖŚŠŜŞŠßŦŢ Ţ̣Ţ̣Ú ÙÛ
ÛÙÚÛ ŲŲ̇Ů Ũ ŴŴŴ̃ Ŵ̇ Ŵ̋ÝŶŸŸ̇ŹŻŽ
aabcdeffgghijklmnopqrstuvuwxyyz
áâàäãåąåãæóáöäàäąóàćčçĉċòďdéěē
ëèêēĕ̇ęģĝ ġ ğ ġ̇ ĝ ġ̇ gh ḥ íĩìíïĩĭiịĩijĵ ĵ̣ k̂ í f̣̂ ḷ ł ḷ ńń
ňńñóǫ́óôòöõōøœðþf̣̂ ŕ̃ ŗ̥ ś š ŝ ş š ß ŧ ţ̣̂ ţ ţ ú ú
û û ù ũ ù ų ů ů ũ ŵ ŵ ŵ̃ ŵ̇ ŵ̋ ẉ̂̊ ý ŷ ÿ ÿ̇ ý ĝ ẙ ĝ̇ ź ż ž
fb ff fh fi fj fk fl ffb ffh ffi ffj ffk ffl
¢ ¤ $ £ ¢ £ ₹ € ¥ ¢ ¤ $ £ ¢ £ ₹ € ¥
12345678900123456789 00
0123456789   0123456789
0123456789/0123456789 ½ ⅓ ⅔ ¼ ¾ ⅜ ⅝ ⅛
.,:;…·‚·¡!¿?*#"'\/()[]{}()—-----
‹›«»‹›«»„""''‚'
+ − × ÷ = ≈ ≠ ± ¬ > < ≥ ≤ % ‰ ∞ ∫ ∂ ∏ √ ∑ ◊ | | & & ¶ § @
@ © ℗ ™ ℮ ° ^ ↑ Δ Ω µ π ↑ ↗ → ↘ ↓ ↙ ← ↖ · · · ·
·´˘ˇ¸ˆ˙¨˝`¯˛˚~˜¸‸··

Graviola

Thin Light Book Regular **Medium** **Bold** **Heavy** **Black**
Thin *Light* *Book* *Regular* *Medium* ***Bold*** ***Heavy*** ***Black***

A Graviola é uma tipografia macia e amistosa. Suas características
mais marcantes são o desenho semiarredondado dos terminais em
gancho e os traços diagonais em curva, que lhe conferem uma
personalidade amigável.

Sua família consiste em 16 fontes, do Thin ao Black mais itálicos
verdadeiros. Possui desenhos alternativos para os caracteres
avwy+ ouwy e Gg& Gg&, que podem ser acessados pelo usuário
através de dois stylistic sets.

Cada fonte contém mais de 530 glifos, que podem compor textos
em mais de 90 idiomas. A Graviola foi publicada pela Harbor Type
em 2014.

39

Tipos Brasileiros
The Brazilian type scene

TEXT BY YVES PETERS

My first encounter with the Brazilian type design scene in São Paulo gave me the impression that quite a bit is happening on that front, with new talent emerging and interesting work being released. The Tipos Latinos biennial (see p. 144) leaves no doubt that this is a golden age for Latin American typography. Brazil has become an integral part of the vibrant typographic culture Latin America has had for over a decade now.

The local type scene is still very young. Like many other countries, Brazil has imported type from Europe and the United States for centuries. Isabella Ribeiro Aragão's research on the history of Funtimod – Fundição de Tipos Modernos (Modern Type Foundry), the largest and first industrial-scale type manufacturer with a national reach, seems to corroborate that there were little to no Brazilian original typefaces. Digital font design started in Brazil in the late 1980s with Tony de Marco. In the early 1990s the proliferation of the personal computer gave Brazilian designers the opportunity to explore this new medium for the first time. Much of this early production is documented in the book *Fontes digitais brasileiras: de 1989 a 2001*, edited by Priscila Lena Farias and Gustavo Piqueira.

Almost all the designers I have spoken with discovered typeface design by accident. In 2004, after acquiring Fontographer and discovering a virtual community of type designers, Marconi Lima of TypeFolio decided to study typography and make his first foray into typeface design. This resulted in Adriane, a serif text family released in 2007. Christopher Hammerschmidt designed his first basic family of text typefaces as the final project for his undergraduate degree in Graphic Arts. In collaboration with Marconi Lima, five years and many improvements later it was released as Capitolina by

TypeFolio in 2015. Henrique Beier of Harbor Type first came into contact with type design in college, where the prospect of designing something as pure as letterforms stuck with him. By chance, Luisa Baeta took a workshop with Eduardo Berliner, the first Brazilian graduate from MATD at Reading. Diego Maldonado of Just in Type had a great Editorial Design teacher who made him study typography. When Tony de Marco saw his early experiments on Flickr, he offered Diego to be his design apprentice.

There are many more similar stories to be told about Brazilians getting into typeface design. One thread that connects them all is that they are a testimony to the personal drive, dedication and commitment of designers who are developing and perfecting their work.

Despite the fact that there are really good Latin American type designers out there, Daniel Sabino of Blackletra feels many still have a lot to learn concerning aesthetic and technical qualities and the behaviour of the type market. As soon as they discover it is possible to make a living producing type, some designers tend to lower their quality standards and slash prices in an effort to publish greater volumes in the hopes of making more money.

Big strides have been made in design education, and typographic

Stevie Sans by Marconi Lima reviewed

culture is spreading fast. Through teaching and workshops, type designers try to instil in students a love and awareness for typography, which in turn makes them more conscious about type. Year after year, activities promoting typographic education and typeface design have brought Brazil the educational project Tipocracia, events such as Tipos Latinos and Dia-Tipo, and local writers such as Priscila Lena Farias and Claudio Rocha, gradually breaking down any remaining barriers. Thanks to the internet, an incredible amount of knowledge is at hand, which has allowed Brazilian type designers to outgrow pure experimentalism and join the professional global font market.

Designers mention the need to educate users about type licences. Sales are made mostly to people and agencies outside the country and even the continent. It is the responsibility of educators and type designers themselves to address the problem of piracy and create an environment where type design is valued and properly compensated.

The new generation is still discovering a new and exciting world that was unknown to them, with no tradition to weigh them down. This near absence of type history makes Brazilian designers less inclined to respect typographic dogmas or slavishly follow historical models, giving them

the freedom to try out conceptual ideas and mix things up without getting too worried about what can or cannot be done. Even more so, this generation of typeface designers feels that they are in the exciting position of shaping what the world will eventually perceive as Brazilian typography.

There is an impressive variety of work informed by the eclectic interests of the type designers, with wonderful vernacular influences that are particular to Brazilian culture – see Buggy / Tipos do Acaso and Fátima Finizola, for example. Others interpret international influences in new and surprising ways. Whereas early Brazilian typefaces were often experimental and mainly focused on display type, the field is coming into its own. Well-produced, high-quality type families are being released for both text and display use. The latest editions of the Tipos Latinos exhibition attest to Brazil's representation and growing importance in Latin American type design. Tony & Caio de Marco's intricate ornamental typeface Samba™ was one of the winners selected during Linotype's 2003 International Type Design Contest, and Daniel Sabino has won two Certificates of Excellence in Type Design – in 2013 for the energetic serif face Karol, and in 2015 for the stunning script Haltrix. In the custom font market, the Brazilian office of Dalton Maag plays a major role.

Inspired by the intercontinental success of Latin American foundries like Latinotype and Sudtipos, Brazilian type designers are maturing and starting to be noticed as serious players in the market. Brazilian designers can fall back on their heritage and visual culture to achieve this. By incorporating the Brazilian joie-de-vivre and playfulness into their designs, they can offer truly unique typefaces to a global audience. Fabio Haag makes the perfect concluding statement: "Above all, we must be humble and understand that in typeface design, we never ever stop learning. We must celebrate where we are, but we must always look forward."

Reprinted with the kind permission of Monotype GmbH www.monotype.com. This is an edited version of a text originally published on www.fontshop.com/content/fontes-brasileiras-the-brazilian-type-scene.

Fabio Haag,
Dalton Maag

Rio 2016, Fabio Haag, Fernando Caro, Marconi Lima, Francesca Bolognini, Bianca Berning & Paolo Mazzetti, 2012

dama do condadinho bacana

κάτι διασκεδαστικό

Peter Cushing lives just down the street

milkmaid

unapplauded penguin

pizzottella

an entourage of revellers

a nimble trickster

I prefer "eccentric"

Alberto Santos-Dumont, o pai da aviação!

a QUIRKY skeleton

with a crisp finish

intricate contraptions & flying machines

a grotesque for the weekend

Franklin in flip-flops

Luisa Baeta

Arlecchino, Luisa Baeta's student project for the MATD in Reading, 2011
Bligh typeface by Luisa Baeta for Dalton Maag, 2015

Adriane Text
ADRIANE LUX
Adriane Swash
Stevie Gothic
Madre Script

Marconi Lima, Typefolio

Retail typefaces of TypeFolio Digital Foundry, designed by Marconi Lima

Christopher Hammerschmidt, Typefolio

Capitolina by Christopher Hammerschmidt, a typeface for editorial design that is also suitable for texts in digital environments, 2015

Daniel Sabino, Blackletra

Random letters (mostly from the Silva type family) by Daniel Sabino

**Rodrigo Saiani,
plau.co**

Tenez, serif display typeface designed by Rodrigo
Saiani, selected for the Tipos Latinos biennial

PLAU, FOR THE FIFTH TIME, PROUDLY INTRODUCES

its latest typeface creation

the Grand Slam family

TENEZ

ORGANIC DIDONE IN 8 STYLES

LIGHTLY INSPIRED BY THE ELEGANT SPORT OF TENNIS

LATIN LANGUAGES SUPPORT

124

unapologetic

exquisite

DISPLAY

DESIGNED BY

RODRIGO SAIANI

WITH THE LUXURIOUS GRAPHIC DESIGN OF

CAMPOI · FLORA · GALC · DOMI & DANI

Don Quixote

meðfram fjölförnum þjóðvegum

The typecasters

Zhruba 57% území Brazílie zaujímají lesy

Masa ciała 1775,9 ± 120,1 g (n=59)

LEIPZIGER STRAßE

Anita & Giuseppe have just got married

MEDIALUNA DE JAMÓN Y QUESO: $45

Butterflies

they fill my guts when I look in your eyes

Dwight Schrute

Baby pandas wrestle with their keeper

My xylophone loves me

accidental stormtrooper

Four secrets goldfish are hiding

Renowned human rights lawyer marries actor

Henrique Beier, Harbor Type

Graviola by Henrique Beier (left), a soft and friendly sans-serif typeface, 2014
Garibaldi by Henrique Beier, a neo-humanist type family derived from
the broad-nib pen, 2015

Befter Sans

aaaaa**aaaaaaaaaaa**aaaaaa

Diego Maldonado, Just in Type

Befter Sans by Diego Maldonado, a contemporary look on classic type, 2016
Sorvettero by Diego Maldonado, a typeface inspired by wood signs in a small
city in Brazil, 2015

40
Floating
Letters

TEXT BY FERNANDA MARTINS

The wooden riverboats of the Amazonian region have a special distinguishing mark: colourfully-painted letters that strongly resemble decorative 19th-century type. The Floating Letters project has aimed to increase awareness about this practice since 2004.

**Photos: Letrasqflutuam
(Fernanda Martins and
Sâmia Batista)**

What was originally a design research project that collected images of local lettering later delved deeper, identifying the professionals involved in this craft, their techniques and ways of handing the craft down to future generations. These artisans call themselves letter "openers", and the act of "opening" or inscribing letters on a boat is a traditional skill found in many Amazonian communities – especially those directly connected to the Amazon basin. Even today, besides on boats, the typical lettering can be found on façades of commercial buildings in Amazonian municipalities. Even though it is a long-standing tradition, the craft is an aspect of our culture that is still poorly recognized and documented, and therefore remains marginal and invisible.

Boat letter "openers" are folk artists who receive their assignments from boat owners who intend to make their vessels unique and special, engaged in dialogue with their passengers. These are ordinary men of the river, influenced not only by the flow of the river but also by the constant flow of contemporary images and media.

As the Floating Letters project intends to draw attention to this intangible Amazonian heritage, bringing new meanings to the tradition while helping to increase the incomes of the artisans that continue it, an online store for their products is in the works. Invitations to speak at academic and non-academic conferences and seminars have come in, and in 2016 we started offering workshops at public schools and book fairs. A documentary promoting the craft was released in 2014 and is available online. We recently returned to the state of Pará in northern Brazil and are currently focusing on the island of Marajó to better understand how the craft is practiced in situ. A new film is scheduled for release in July 2017.

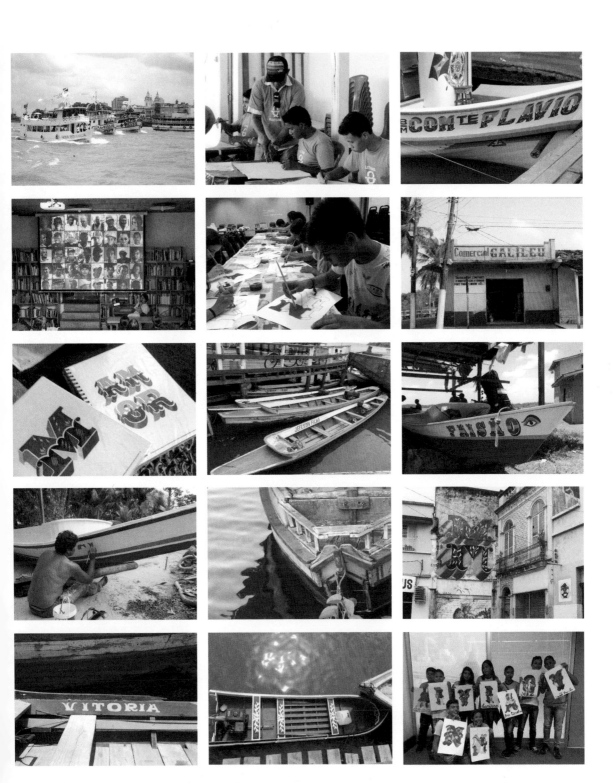

41
Letters from Salamanca

TEXT & PHOTOS BY ANDREU BALIUS

Salamanca is a beautiful city located in the western Castilian plateau. It is famous for its Renaissance buildings, the tasty Iberian ham and, of course, its university building, one of the oldest in Europe.

"They say that the original red colour comes from bull blood, and signs have been painted this way for centuries."

One of the most amazing things you can look at when walking through the narrow streets of the old town are the large number of lettering signs painted directly on the stone surfaces of the buildings – reddish roman letters on yellow stones from Villamayor quarry.

They say that the original red colour comes from bull blood, and signs have been painted this way for centuries. In fact, some lettering signs were painted as far back as the 16th century.

From the university's very beginnings in the Castilian Renaissance period, nobles and clerics who got licensed used to celebrate with sumptuous banquets and bullfights. They also had the right to draw their families' noble names on the faculty walls as a way to honour themselves as doctors. Bull blood and natural pigments were used for this purpose.

While some of the lettering signs are works of gracefulness, others are good examples of total madness. Not always was a good letterer commissioned to do the job. In fact, improvisation seems to be part of the way letters were composed and painted one after the other.

Old painted bits appear below more recent work in a sort of messy, multi-layered pattern that converts some corners in gorgeous pieces of random artwork.

There are two different sorts of styles within the extensive range of roman letters: roman capitals with very strong, high contrast (approaching Didone style), and more classical letters with a more rounded, humanist flavour. The use of uppercase is general in all cases.

A certain *horror vacui* in the way the letters are arranged is a feature quite close to the characteristics of the local Renaissance architectural style, generating an organic texture in word composition that converts words and groups of letters to something close to a brand.

Nowadays this lettering tradition has become a "source" for new signboards that are being painted within the city. In fact, this lettering style has become an element for the city's identity.

ARISTIDS ROY.
REPVBLICÆ PANAMENSIS
PRÆSES
VNIVERSITATEM SVAM
VISITAVIT
A.D. MCMLXXIX

42
Horn ~~Please~~
No Thank You!

TEXT & PHOTOS BY ROB KELLER

The words "Horn Please*" or "Horn OK Please" are very common on every shape and size of truck throughout India. Often highly decorative, the words are now being obliterated from trucks in the state of Maharashtra following a government regulation aimed at reducing noise pollution.

* This phrase is so prevalent that two books identically titled *Horn Please* (one by Dan Eckstein, the other by Pawan Jain & Divya Jain), both about India's painted trucks, were published in 2014. Moreover, a short documentary on Indian truck art also titled *Horn Please* was released in 2013.

The exact origin of why this phrase is so ubiquitous is a mystery; some say the "OK" stood for "On Kerosene" so one would take extra caution around these unsafe trucks. Another theory is that the OK once had a lightbulb above it, which the driver would turn on during the night when there was no oncoming traffic stating it was OK to pass. The "Horn Please" comes from a combination of issues (mainly due to narrow or poor roads) but gives clear instructions to honk before overtaking. In any case, these slogans have been widely used for decades and are now an internationally recognized feature of Indian trucks.

As designers, our primary interest in this topic comes from the art on these trucks and how they are mostly still completely hand-painted, featuring fancy lettering, bright colors and ornate decorations. The unique treatments for each truck show the driver's or company's personality and contribute significantly to India's vibrant image. But thanks to the falling costs and increased speed of modernization – chiefly thanks to quick typesetting and digital printing – lettering artists are rapidly losing work. This trend began with shop signs, but is now beginning to affect trucks as well.

Roads paved with good intentions ...

Then in April 2015 the Maharashtra State government took the progressive step of banning the words "Horn OK Please" on trucks. This new prohibition only applies to trucks registered in this state; it is not a nationwide law (yet). Their motivation for this law stemmed from the fact that everyone is constantly honking when driving, and they believe that this painted phrase on trucks only encourages excess noise.

"It gives licence to motorists to honk unnecessarily and there have been numerous complaints of excessive honking in silence zones such as near hospitals, schools and colleges. We have, therefore, decided to impose a ban on the use of this phrase," a senior official from the transport commissioner's office told Somit Sen of *The Economic Times* on 1 May 2015, adding that the ban would also help reduce noise pollution.

Filling the void?

Even though truckers can now be stopped by the police and fined for still having these words on their trucks, the ban hasn't fully caught on

yet. But as of the end of the year, more and more trucks around Mumbai are beginning to cover up their lettering. The most common "fix" is to simply put tape over the words, but others are taking an extra step and crudely painting over it. Very rarely are people utilizing this opportunity to redesign and repaint the back of their truck. But my hope is that when it comes times to paint or repaint these vehicles, there will still be interest in applying creativity and personality to them, and not simply leaving an empty hole where Horn OK Please was once written. I optimistically predict more "Don't be Horny" and "India is Great" paintings to start appearing soon in Maharashtra.

"The unique treatments for each truck
show the driver's or company's personality
and contribute significantly to India's
vibrant image."

43
Grafist 20:
Istanbul at the start of a new wave of interest in graphic design

TEXT BY CHRISTOPHER ÇOLAK

Grafist, Istanbul Graphic Design Week, has been organized every year since 1997 by the graphic design department at Mimar Sinan Fine Arts University's Fine Arts Faculty in conjunction with the Turkish Society of Graphic Designers (GMK). Grafist aims to create a multidisciplinary design forum in which students have a chance to interact with famous designers. With its series of seminars, workshops and exhibitions, Grafist is one of the city's leading design events, interesting for both students and professionals alike.

2016 marked the 90th anniversary since the establishment of Mimar Sinan Fine Arts University and the 20th annual Grafist. Grafist 20 was also celebrated with the 19 April opening of the MSFAU Centre of Graphic Design Application & Research, located in a sweet old vernacular Istanbul apartment in Cihangir.

Through the efforts of Ayşegül İzer (head of the graphic design department at Mimar Sinan University), Sinan Niyazioğlu (head of the new research and application centre), Sadık Karamustafa and others, Istanbul has

taken a first step forward to soon having its own graphic design museum. With 20 years of archives from previous Grafist events, the centre's collection contains thousands of design materials, ephemera and historical data from participants from around the world, and every day it continues to grow from personal donations made by local designers

"Grafist has been continuing its journey with selfless and dedicated efforts for 20 years now. Grafist brings the world to Istanbul and delivers Istanbul to the world."
Yeşim Demir Pröhl

Time changes everything, a type installation by Indian street artist Daku, was created as part of the 4th street art festival St+Art in New Delhi in early 2016.

44

Shadow graffiti: "Time changes everything"

Photo: Pranav Gohil

Twenty-five local and international street artists joined the St+Art project, turning the urban landscape of the iconic Lodhi colony area in New Delhi into an open-air gallery.

In his first dynamic, typographic graffiti project, Daku – the initiator of the festival and a graffiti artist who, like Banksy, remains anonymous – ingeniously visualizes the concept of time and its passing by playing with letters and shadows.

The oldest forms of measuring time were sundials used by the Egyptians as early as 1500 BCE; Daku's piece takes that concept to a whole new level. By mounting words perpendicularly on a building façade, thus making them cast an ever-evolving shadow through the day, Daku speaks metaphorically of all the things in life that change over time.

Every day throughout the year this piece comes alive between 9:30 a.m. and 2:30 p.m., after which it disappears with the fading Sun. At noon, when the sun shines directly on the wall, the shadow words become "regular" and most legible. As time passes, the slant of the shadow increases, making the letters slowly fade away as the sun sets; between 15 May and 15 August, when there is no shadow on the wall at all, the installation becomes completely abstract. The words featured in this piece, such as *perception*, *value*, *fame*, *meaning*, or even *reality*, not only speak of the nature of our lives, but also the ephemeral nature of street art, which is constantly changing.

The quintessential black & white oval number signs that have graced houses in the Argentine capital since the early 20th century are slowly disappearing. Can a digitized typeface help save them?

45
Numbering Buenos Aires: Enamel house numbers inspire a new typeface

TEXT BY DARÍO MUHAFARA & MARÍA LAURA NIETO

From the very beginning, the numbering system followed a set of guidelines: standard oval enamel signs, black numbers on white, mounted at a designated place next to the door. In reality, the signs can be seen on most, but not all houses. Unfortunately, a rising number of the plaques have been changed according to the owners' taste. When we tried to restore one for our home, we found the last craft workshop and learned about its cultural history. If house-numbering systems are site specific, we wanted to value and keep the Buenos Aires system alive. With this we launched into research and created a typeface aimed at recovering these vernacular signs.

Past ...
The Buenos Aires system was born under a 1894 law that stated every house door in the new city must bear an enamel number issued by the gov-

1 – Buenos Aires' white oval enamel house numbers
2 – An enamel sign ready for cleaning and the final bake
3 – The last workshop

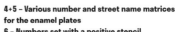

4

5

4+5 – Various number and street name matrices
for the enamel plates
6 – Numbers set with a positive stencil

ernment. Just a few years earlier, the city was made an autonomous district and the city limits were enlarged. At the same time a new urban plan was designed based on the modernist approach of homogeneous urbanization. By the first half of the 20th century, Buenos Aires had become a cosmopolitan, integrated metropolis and every doorway had its own new enamel sign.

Since the mid-19th century, the most common typefaces used throughout Argentina were based on Bodoni. This typographical taste was consolidated in what people were accustomed to seeing every day, such as newspapers, signposts, printed numbers and, of course, enamel house numbers.

... and present

Each workshop that made house signs interpreted the numbers in its own (or rather its own signmaker's) style. The Didone spirit was maintained, with natural variations in craftsmanship, personal flavour and technical skill. In fact the last workshop to remain in business still cuts the matrices by hand.

By walking through the city and talking with the last workshop signmaker, we rediscovered and digitized a typeface that brings together what we believe are the five most representative city number styles: *Contrastada*, *Oficial*, *Turri*, *La Pilarica* and *Recoleta*, all with positive and negative stencils.

We wanted to bring these emblematic numbers back to the present, as part of our common cultural memory and identity. These numbers have a history and we wanted to tell something about them.

012345

0123456

0123456

0123456

0123456

0123 4

6

46
New Zealand flag consideration project

TEXT BY DIONYSIS LIVANIS

Some people don't understand why New Zealand was considering changing its flag, and others don't understand why New Zealand did not change it in the end. As designers we can see this project as a branding exercise. Creating the flag of a country is not much different from creating the symbol of an organization. However, a flag that expresses and even influences a country's collective identity is a much more complicated and emotionally charged issue.

In March 2016, New Zealand held a referendum for its people to decide between the current flag of the country and a new one, the Silver Fern designed by architect Kyle Lockwood. This was the second referendum about the matter; a few months earlier in another public vote New Zealanders selected their preference from a choice of five designs.

There were many rational reasons why the country needed to change its flag. As Prime Minister John Key argued, "the design of the New Zealand flag symbolizes a colonial and post-colonial era whose time has passed". Supporters of the change thought it was time for the country to have a flag with its own symbols rather than the British Blue Ensign. Another more practical reason was the very frequent confusion between the New Zealand and Australian flag.

The public debate and final vote proved that when it comes to their history and sense of identity, people are much less rational and far more emotional. For the supporters of the current flag it was a matter of staying true to their past; the question was not what the individual elements on the flag symbolize, but what the flag as a whole has come to represent.

The first referendum started on 20 November 2015 with voting closing three weeks later on 11 December 2015.

The second referendum started on 3 March 2016 with voting closing three weeks later on 24 March 2016.

On 24 March 2016, the preliminary results of the second referendum were announced with the current flag winning 56.7% compared to 43.3% for the new flag.

1 – Designed by Kyle Lockwood
2 – Designed by Aaron Dustin
3 – Designed by Alofi Kanter
4 – Designed by Kyle Lockwood
5 – Designed by Andrew Fyfe

47

The Łódź-Orwo Collection

CAPTIONS BY JAN KUBASIEWICZ

The Łódź-Orwo Collection
is a set of two hundred
35-mm slides documenting
urban typography and visual
communication in the city
of Łódź, Poland, in the late
1970s. The slides were part
of a bigger collection, which
originated from a student
research project at the
Academy of Fine Arts in Łódź.

1

2

3

Students were asked to capture the urban visual environment, samples of typography, signage and more on 35-mm transparency slides. Over the years the collection grew to several hundred, but when project leader Jan Kubasiewicz defected to the United States in 1987, the whole archive of prints, books, photographs and slides was left behind in his studio. Over the years the archive was moved from place to place, and as a result the slides, together with other items, were assumed lost.

But a break came in 2009, when a single box of two hundred slides from that collection was unexpectedly rediscovered. The current name of the collection refers to the Orwo-Chrom brand; "made in GDR", it was the only diapositive transparency film stock available in Poland (or any of the Eastern Bloc countries) at the time.

Although only a fraction of the original collection has been preserved after all these years, its documentary value is enormous. In terms of typography, it presents a unique dialogue between the large propaganda billboards and shop windows of small "private enterprises", between posters promoting film premieres and ads for local discos and ironing services – the everyday life of a city as contained in its typography.

Advertising mural for government-owned *Prexer* (1), a manufacturer of military optical equipment, is a good case study of large-budget corporate marketing treated as "propaganda". The murals functioned more as public relation announcements than advertising. Consumer products did not really need any advertising. However, government-owned brands wanted visibility. The *Prexer* mural is a purely abstract visual solution reminiscent of best examples of Op Art by Alberto Biasi or Vasarely, and has nothing to do with the direct advertising of the consumer products they manufactured, such as film and slide projectors. On many occasions, the fashionable Op Art visual vocabulary became an adopted strategy in advertising various government-owned companies, big and small, from textile manufacturer *Ortal* (3) to a *Kaskada* restaurant (2).

4

5

"At Every Workplace We Forge the Future of Poland" (4) is a display panel designed with a minimalistic approach to typographical composition: sans-serif Helvetica font, asymmetrical, flush left type arrangement, supported by abstract rectangular shapes of vibrant colour demanding attention. Helvetica was a novelty font at the time, imported as Letraset sheets (for designers that meant "progress" over Akzidenz Grotesk). Type was enlarged photographically, prepared as stencils, and painted manually. The Letraset sheets did not include Polish diacritical marks, and that became a laboratory for type design "experiments" – often very poorly executed.

The panel "Good Work" (5) is an amazing example of a search for originality and uniqueness in font selection that went too far. The font known today as "Archetype Catalogue Solid" (The Foundry) was originally des igned by Wim Crouwel in 1970 specifically for the branding of Claes Oldenburg's exhibition at the Stedelijk Museum in Amsterdam, Holland. An unknown designer who appropriated the font to that propaganda slogan, provided – intentionally or not – a rather sarcastic overtone to the message. The modular and organically shaped graphemes of Crouwel's design are paired with a grid of squares with slightly rounded corners and placed on large-scale panels behind a chain-link fence.

8

6

The concert promotion for international celebrity Charles Aznavour is a 3-dimensional structure made of plywood (an abstract sculpture itself) on which a number of posters were mounted (6). On the adjacent structure fencing the main sculpture, the photographic poster of Aznavour is mounted next to the poster of Maria Limonta, another international celebrity performer. Her portrait-based poster was designed by Waldemar Świerzy, a prominent member of the Polish School of Posters.

On the billboard advertising the 1976 American feature film *The Battle of Midway* (7) a local designer freely appropriated graphic components of the original poster for the Polish release (designed by Andrzej Krajewski, another member of the Polish School of Poster elite). Such practice was rather widespread. Many local announcements were executed by local artists following the visual language of well-known celebrity designers. However, many craftsmen letterers tried to preserve their autonomy, as in the case of the local poster for the 1976 Martin Scorsese film *Taxi Driver* (8).

7

9

On many occasions, announcements of local cultural
events became informal interpretations of pop-art visual
vocabulary executed free-hand by community organizers,
not necessarily designers (9).

11

12

In contrast, new entrepreneurs, with a lot of courage, hope and funding, identified with the American dream of self-made millionaires. Their typographical identity referred stylistically to the 19th century American typography of the "wanted" posters (10), so well documented in the Rob Roy Kelly Collection at the University of Texas at Austin, or the most fashionable Push Pin Studio-inspired ITC fonts. The signage of such storefronts as "Tali Jeans" (11), "Jeans Boutique, *Dernier Cri*" (12) not only perfectly represented the merchandise – jeans, apparel, accessories – but aggressively disconnected their visual language from an elegant European tradition in favour of the visual manifestation of the "nouveau riche" in the American style.

48
Authoritative Design

TEXT BY REZA ABEDINI

Authoritative Design is a collaborative design project based on a collection of over 300 contemporary posters by 45 Iranian designers. It has been displayed in galleries and important international museums ranging far and wide, from Tehran and Berlin to Rome and Beirut. The most recent exhibition was held in Vienna, Austria, in September 2016.

Perhaps the most difficult and complex design project is a poster or book for a visual artist or another designer. Of course, if we approach this simplistically, we might produce something similar to what most museums and especially galleries do: a picture of the artist's most famous work, the name of the artist in bold at the top or bottom of the poster (but probably the top), the rest of the information below it in a safe and basic layout (so as to not disturb the image), plus several big and small logos in order of importance (how much money they have paid or are receiving) on the left or right of the poster and – done!

Design becomes difficult when we consider graphic design and the designer as more and decide to leave the shallow, rusted and confusing definition of "designer = problem solver" behind. In fact, the only time these issues arise in graphic design is when we are dealing with a designer/author.

Often the best output from designer-problem solvers is a visual reaction to the artist's atmosphere that has been (conservatively) presented using the artist's work itself.

The truth is, if we take even a quick look at the history of graphic design and the works of notable contemporary designers, even those who disagree with having a personal visual style and accent, we find that their entire body of work is clearly recognizable and this is solely because the designer's unique world view is manifested in their works through their particular use of elements and techniques, making their works their own. This means they put concepts through their own mental filters and in some ways redefine them.

This process is very complicated, of course. The authoritative designer must face a new set of information and conditions about the subject of design and pass it through their own filters to gain their own, undoubtedly contemporary understanding. At the same time, they need to consider the function of their chosen medium. And they need to be creative. To me, the combination of all of these is what creativity is.

On the other hand, it must be known that being authoritative is not a conscious state and not one that can be feigned. Any attempt to force a visual style will create shallow and superficial results in the designer's work.

Authoritative designers first develop their own visual world and familiarize others with it, and then create their pieces in this same world.

Having a personal style begins at the commentary and interpretation of concepts, and thus requires a deep understanding of current affairs, history, society and culture. One sign of an authoritative designer is that all the elements and phenomena in his or her work are assimilated, in sync, and come from the same world. This cannot happen unless in a completely natural and unconscious manner.

The important question is: what is the position of a designer who is going

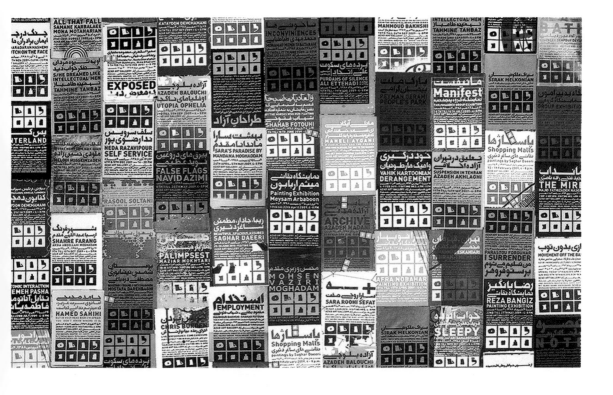

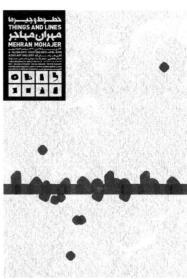

1

2

3

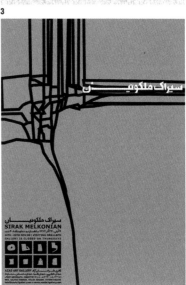

4

5

6

1 – Studio Kargah: Palimpses, 2011
2 – Morteza Mahallati: The End Of Purity, 2011
3 – StudioKargah: Things and Lines, 2012
4 – Sanaz Soltani: Yesterday, Today, 2014
5 – Vahid Erfanian: I Am Lost, 2013
6 – Reza Abedini: Sirak Melkonian, 2008
7 – Vahid Erfanian: The Winter Video Art (Iran & Japan), 2014
8 – Mojtaba Adibi: From Land, 2014
9 – Homa Delvaray: Die Iranische Weltanschauung, 2011
10 – Rambod Vala: All Of The "T" Men, 2010
11 – Golnaz Esmaeili: I'm Not Sleep, Just Closed My Eyes, 2010
12 – Hussein Nasseredine: Free Zone, 2014

7

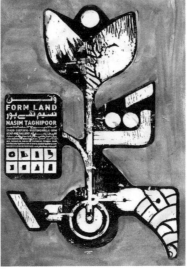

8

9

10

11

12

The Azad Art Gallery Collaborative Design Project is the result of a collaborative endeavour between Reza Abedini, a group of young Iranian graphic designers and the Azad Art Gallery in Tehran in 2008.
Each individual poster (975 × 675 mm) has three functions: poster, invitation (by folding) and small catalogue (back side of each poster). Each season the collection of small catalogues is bound together to make a seasonal catalogue.

Idea, creative direction and design: Reza Abedini; art direction and design: Aria Kasaei; coordination: Studio Kargah

13

14

15

to design a poster for another artist? Must the designer completely drown themselves in the visual language and viewpoint of the artist? Or must they present their own interpretation of the artist and their works? In both cases, the poster must clearly convey the intended message and function as communication of the artist's or the exhibition's intentions.

We have chosen the second method. And we're convinced that it is the correct way. This collection is the result of a 2008 movement that began surrounding this very question. The current collection is a selection of a much bigger body of works and is the result of the efforts of tens of graphic designers, executive producers and at least three art directors. On the other hand, hours of conversations in different meetings to explain and justify the artists (initially) and discussions and consultations with designers on finding the right direction are among the things that made it possible for this substantial project to exist and continue to grow.

At the beginning of this project, in addition to a technical framework, we defined few artistic and aesthetical boundaries and tried our best to stay faithful to them: simplicity and clear communication; choosing designers who are in some way familiar with Iranian art; choosing designers who are familiar with Persian script and typography; keeping the main format of information in one of the designed boxes; making an effort to introduce young and contemporary designers; and making an effort to introduce visual language that is regional/traditional, yet still contemporary.

Insistence on continuing this method, which was met with complete support from the Azad Art Gallery in Tehran, has resulted in a positive influence in the artistic atmosphere of the city and its galleries. It is rare to find a gallery in Tehran nowadays that does not have an art director and is not concerned with having a unique visual identity. Furthermore, participating in this project and designing a poster for Azad Art Gallery is considered an advantage for young contemporary designers.

16

17

18

19

20

21

13 – Omid Nemalhabib: Another Side, 2012
14 – Shahrzad Changlavaee: Sara's Paradise, 2009
15 – Sanaz Soltani: Yazesh, 2015
16 – Mohammad Reza Abdolali: Gradual Fade Of A Smile, 2013
17 – Iman Raad: Shopping Malls, 2009
18 – Aria Kasaei: The Second Scene Of The Adventure, 2014
19 – Farhad Fozouni: Mr President, 2015
20 – Behrad Javanbakht: Locking Horn, 2014
21 – Shahrzad Changlavaee: Chasing, 2014

22

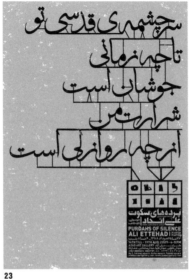

23

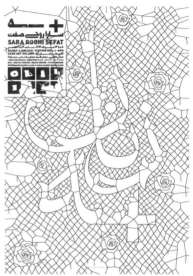

24

25

26

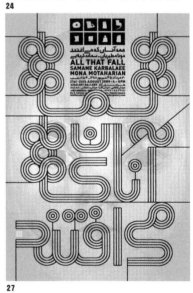

27

22 – Mohammad Khodashenas: Self And Selfless, 2015
23 – Aria Kasaei: Purdahs of Silence, 2009
24 – Masoud Morgan: Sara Roohi Sefat, 2010
25 – Mohammad Reza Abdolali: Retail and Whole Sale of Your Family Photos, 2015
26 – Behrad Javanbakht: I Bestow A Look Upon You, 2012
27 – Mohammad Reza Abdolali: All That Fall, 2009
28 – Peyman Pourhossein: Afternoon Tea Will Be Provided, 2012
29 – Peyman Pourhossein: Tehran – The Hero, 2010
30 – Omid Nemalhabib: Gone Wild, 2015
31 – Sanaz Soltani: Closed, 2013
32 – Reza Babajani: Khawarnaq, 2014
33 – Reza Abedini: Tarahane Azad, 2010

28

29

30

31

32

33

When confronted with photocomposition, computers, videos, & technology in general, the only chance calligraphy has to survive is to remain, above all creative, exclusive, unique, exclusive & very plastic!

JEAN LARCHER

1 – Scriptores, volume 7 no. 3/4. Coll. Alan Marshall, Musée de l'Imprimerie, Lyon
2 – Plouf Black, Hollenstein phototypesetting. Musée de l'Imprimerie, Lyon

exclusivité hollenstein
plouf black
création jean larcher

2

Most will remember Jean Larcher for the masterful curves that he developed in a flourished Spencerian script. Probably the best 20th century French calligrapher in this style, Larcher primarily focused on expanding awareness about calligraphy by holding workshops and talks throughout the world in his final years.

49

Jean Larcher (1947–2015): A visual obituary

TEXT BY JEAN-BAPTISTE LEVÉE

Only in 2014 did he seem to want to epitomize his achievements in a voluminous book that would gather the sum of his experiences. *Character Traits* is a 500-page potpourri of various calligraphic styles, mostly using maxims and mottos as an excuse for calligraphic entertainment. If the shape of the exercise is far from being a novelty, one can gladly welcome it as a partial archive of his hand.

That is what most will remember Larcher for. Few will recall his previous life: a less settled, more energetic style he practiced during the 1970s and 1980s. The young and fierce Larcher was then a supporter of Op Art and geometrical patterns, of which he published a handful of compendia at Dover Publications and even a manifesto in the shape of a book, *About Typography, for a New One* (1976). Larcher's type designs, released by the now-defunct phototypesetting company Hollenstein, were miles away from his later classical style. Odd names such as Crayon, Menhir and Guapo show that this young man was fascinated by the emerging graphic styles of North America, which he dreamed of importing to France. His lettering work was no different: colourful, cheeky, geometric. Let's remember their author as such: bright and witty, a trait that shall now go on forever.

3 – Season's greetings, 2003. Coll. Alan Marshall, Musée de l'Imprimerie, Lyon
4 – "Pop message" (Goodbye). Coll. Alan Marshall, Musée de l'Imprimerie, Lyon
5 – Menhir 8, Hollenstein phototypesetting. Musée de l'Imprimerie, Lyon

3

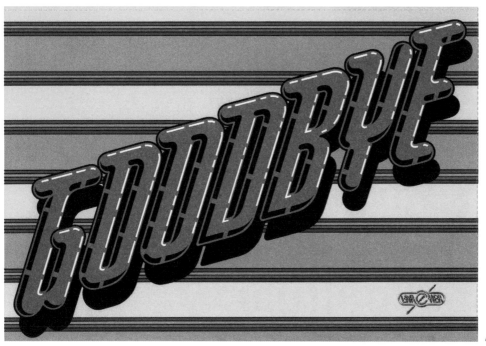

4

exclusivité hollenstein
menhir 8
création jean larcher

ABCCDEEFGHI
JKLMNOPQR
STUVWXYZ
ÆŒÇÇ&¿/*""()
%Ø ‾""˜°'Æ¡?¿!'".:_
1234567890

1

ARK

Number 46 Spring 1970 5/- $1.25

The New Avant Garde part two

As a former member of the Royal Shakespeare Company, Alan Rickman was best known for his film performances, including leading roles in *Die Hard*, *Robin Hood: Prince of Thieves* and the *Harry Potter* series. Less well-known was his previous incarnation as a graphic designer.

50
Alan Rickman (1946–2016)

TEXT BY TEAL TRIGGS

"Working on ARK came at
an important time for me.
In retrospect, I could feel
my wings already beginning
to stretch in other directions."

Alan Rickman studied graphic design at Chelsea School of Art and later at the Royal College of Art between 1968 and 1969 before leaving to form a graphic design studio in Soho, London, with his fellow students. Here he worked as a jobbing designer for three years prior to entering the Royal Academy of Dramatic Arts (RADA).

My contact with Alan Rickman was brief and came about as the result of asking him to contribute to *Graphics-RCA: Fifty Years and Beyond* (2014) – an exhibition and book project co-curated by myself, Richard Doust, Adrian Shaughnessy and Jeff Willis. The aim of the exhibition and accompanying book was to celebrate the achievements of the College's graphic design alumni and faculty while equally exploring what constituted a "typical" graduate of the RCA. To this end we interviewed Rickman, along with Len Deighton, Michele Jannuzzi, Margaret Calvert and Andy Altman, amongst others.

Rickman's work on ARK magazine (the student publication of the time) was highlighted along with his love of visual communication – something that he explained was a "bridge" to the rest of his working life.

TEAL TRIGGS: **Would you say your first ambition was to be a graphic designer?**
ALAN RICKMAN: Yes. Although theatre was always lurking in the background.

As an art school, the Royal College of Art not only provided students with an education, but also fostered a rich social life (through film societies, student union events, parties, etc.). Can you tell us a little about this?
The Graphics department was "annexed" in a huge, echoing room farther down Exhibition Road, adjoined to the V&A. Sadly, we had no daily contact with other disciplines, so I don't remember much in the way of a social life. It was heads down all day.

The RCA journal ARK features heavily in the life of the college, facilitating students in trying new things. You are credited in issues 45 and 46 (1969/1970) of the journal as a copy editor, but also as a writer ["*Interview with Jim Haynes*" (1969) and "*Child's Play*" (1970)]. How important was this to you at the time?
Working on ARK came at an important time for me. In retrospect, I could feel my wings already beginning to stretch in other directions.

ARK

number 45 winter 1969 5 shillings $1.25

This issue's all about the New Avante Garde. So's our next one, out in April.

John Tilbury a———phor——is——es a——bout the new mus————ic. Jim Haynes,

the Sven——ga——li of the dear de——funct Arts Lab, ex————plains how it came to pass.

Ray Connolly gives a Pop what's what. David Adams says Stop Por——nog——ra——

phy in the Un————der ground. Richard and Su Rogers: a prize win————ning

house the plan————ners won't al————low. Gillian Cooke, Honey's queen bee,

tells what's to———mor————row for the ov————er ground mags.

The writing seems to have led to further countercultural publications. How involved were you in the politics of the time?

My design training was used actively on one of the first free left-wing newspapers, *The Notting Hill Herald*. I designed the masthead and worked on the weekly layouts. I was also freelancing on other publications. It was a rich time, politically. And this was all before computers. A lot of indignation, late nights and Letraset.

One of the themes emerging in our research is how graphic design at the RCA has fostered an education which in today's terminology might be understood as "transferable" into other professional careers. What do you feel you gained from your RCA student experience? In what ways did this manifest itself in your later career, both as a designer and actor?

Hindsight means that you can see how the dots joined up along the way. I had already had such a strong training with Edward Wright at Chelsea in terms of his ethics and rigor as a typographer and designer. Coming to the RCA was a consolidation of all that. And now that training is with me every day – in a rehearsal room, an editing suite, in conversations with a cinematographer, a costume, set or titles designer. There's a shorthand.

We understand that after you left the RCA, you set up a studio in Soho. Could you talk a little about how the studio came to be? Who were your collaborators and clients?

It all seems like a 1970s fantasy now. A top floor studio in Berwick Street shared with a photographer, white-washed brick walls and a vaulted glass ceiling. We were a mixed group of designers and illustrators – fellow students from Chelsea – Ann Winterbotham, Tony Phillips, Caroline Brown, and Royston Edwards, along with Penny Jones, who had joined me from Chelsea at the RCA. My job also included hiking around a huge and heavy portfolio to all the art directors. Again, this was BC: Before Computers. We worked on magazine layouts and illustrations, book jackets, album sleeves and advertising. And learned quickly that we had to pay our bills immediately, but that the same rule did not apply to our clients. A constant financial tightrope. It came to a natural finish when I started to work in fringe theatre and then went to RADA, and the others merged with Alan Aldridge at Ink Studios. Happy endings.

First published in: Teal Triggs, Adrian Shaughnessy and Anna Gerber (eds, 2014). *GraphicsRCA: Fifty Years and Beyond*. London: Royal College of Art. Later reproduced online for *Design Observer*, 2014.

1 – *ARK 46*, Spring 1970. Editor Malcolm Winton, Art Editor Darrell Ireland, Adverts Manager Gordon Thompson, Production Manager Joy Law, Copy Editor Alan Rickman, Cover Design John Pasche. © Royal College of Art, reproduced with permission
2 – *ARK 45*, Winter 1969. Editor Malcolm Winton, Art Editor Darrell Ireland, Adverts Manager Penny Jones and Lynda Usher, Production Manager Joy Law, Copy Editor Alan Rickman, Illustration Editor Ray Ogden, Cover Design uncredited. © Royal College of Art, reproduced with permission

51
Some words about Frutiger (1928–2015)

TEXT BY MATTHEW CARTER

1

Adrian Frutiger died on 10 September 2015, in Bern, Switzerland, at the age of 87.

He was born in Unterseen near Interlaken, the son of a weaver. After a local apprenticeship to a compositor he entered the Kunstgewerbeschule in Zürich, where he became especially receptive to the teaching of Alfred Willimann and Walter Käch. Under their instruction he made rubbings of classical inscriptions, wrote calligraphic studies with a broad-edged pen, drew the spaces inside and between letters with white ink on black paper to understand the importance of counterforms in type and, as his final project at the school, made an eighteen-page portfolio to illustrate the historical development of the Latin script by cutting letters with a knife in the long grain of beechwood blocks. This tour de force (it took eight months of work) gave early evidence of the many sides of Frutiger's genius: his historical knowledge, his versatility in the design of different letterforms, and his manual dexterity.

The woodcut portfolio came to the attention of Charles Peignot of the Deberny & Peignot typefoundry in Paris, who hired Frutiger on the strength of it in 1952. The business of the foundry was a traditional one of casting type in metal, but under the farsighted management of Charles Peignot it undertook also the design and manufacture of fonts for the new technology of the Lumitype-Photon photocomposing machine. For metal-casting Frutiger designed Initiales Président (capitals for business cards) and the vigorous script face Ondine. At the urging of Rémy Peignot, Charles' son who had a design office in the foundry, Frutiger turned his attention from display types to designing his first text face, Méridien. It would be hard to find a type design in which the inter-character spacing had been more carefully studied than in Méridien. The open forms of 'e' 'c' and 's' combine with adjacent letters in a way that amounts to a theory of legibility.

To equip the Lumitype machine it was necessary to adapt for photocomposition the standard commercial library of types: Baskerville, Garamond, Bodoni, etc. For a sanserif the obvious choice was Europe (similar to Futura), the foundry's best-selling typeface. But Frutiger's training in Zürich in humanistic letterforms left him unsympathetic to the strict geometry of the Futura model. As a student he had made preliminary designs for a sanserif, in which Käch's influence was manifest. Without knowing how his boss in Paris would react to an alternative proposal, Frutiger went back to his student project and hurriedly added trial characters for a family of weights and widths. Charles Peignot, who loved anything new and original, gave the sanserif both his blessing and its ambitious name, Univers. It was released in metal and Lumitype versions in 1957 to immediate success. Univers, with its meticulous planning and execution, and the elegant clarity of its forms, made Frutiger's reputation international at the age of 29.

To avoid the imprecision of the usual names for typographic weights and widths, not to mention the frustrations of finding equivalents for them in different languages, Frutiger's orderly mind devised a numbering scheme for the 21 members of the Univers family. Although it has been used occasionally elsewhere, and in spite of its logical appeal, the numerical approach has never really caught on. It remains a characteristic of Univers in its time and place.

In 1961, in order to expand his work from type to other forms of graphic design, Frutiger opened his own studio at La Vache Noire in the south of Paris. He was joined there by two colleagues from Switzerland, Bruno Pfäffli and André Gürtler. His time was divided between Deberny & Peignot, the Atelier Frutiger, and teaching at the École Estienne and afterwards at the École National Supérieure des Arts Décoratifs.

In the years that followed Frutiger undertook an astonishing variety of projects. He made an adaptation of Univers for the IBM Composer golfball typewriter, he designed a machine-readable (and human-readable) typeface, OCR-B, for the European Computer Manufacturers' Association for use on checks and other financial documents, he taught at the National Institute of Design in Ahmedabad, India, from which came the design of a Univers-flavored Devanagari

1 – Adrian Frutiger, 2001
2 – Construction of the Frutiger arrow, signage Charles de Gaulle Airport, 1969
3 – Univers typeface family

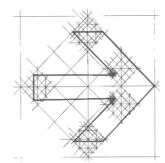

2

typeface. The culture of India and the designers he worked with there retained a special place in his heart.

In 1970 Frutiger was asked to consider the design of signs for the new Paris airport at Roissy. At first it was assumed that Univers would be chosen for setting the signs but Frutiger had second thoughts; the enclosed letterforms of Univers did not lend themselves ideally to clear reading at a distance. A different sanserif with more open forms, Concorde, largely drawn by André Gürtler for line-casting, proved more legible in black (for French) and white (for English) against an illuminated yellow background. The Roissy alphabet, essentially a slightly bolder and more widely spaced version of Concorde, was adopted for the airport and for road signs around it.

Mike Parker, Director of Typographic Development at Mergenthaler Linotype in New York, saw the Roissy signs on a visit to Paris and immediately asked Frutiger to design a version of it for print. Because of his heavy workload, Frutiger delegated much of the adaptation to Hans-Jürg Hunziker, a Swiss designer who had worked at Mergenthaler before joining the Atelier Frutiger in Paris. The decision to give the new sanserif family the name of Frutiger was taken partly for legal reasons, but it seems appropriate; although it was Univers that made Frutiger's reputation, it was the eponymous sanserif that he admitted was his favorite – it reminded him of the work of Constantin Brâncuși – enough said.

Frutiger is best known as a peerless designer of sanserif types, but he was equally at home among serifs. His designs amount to a conspectus of virtually every style of text type in which the Latin alphabet has found expression. In the years after Charles Peignot was no longer in charge of the business that bore his name, and no longer Frutiger's chief patron, Frutiger designed for other clients: Serifa for the Bauersche Giesserei, and Iridium, Icone, Breughel, Versailles, Linotype Centennial, Linotype Didot for D. Stempel AG/Linotype. At various times he also designed a number of custom types, among them faces for BP, the Paris Metro, Shiseido, and

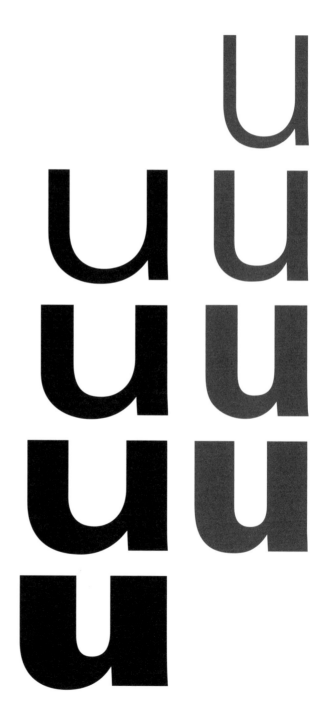

3

4

a digital version of Tiemann for *Die Zeit.*

Frutiger's interest in graphic forms went beyond the alphabet. He was fascinated by symbols, marks that meant something, pictogams, precursors of writing in different cultures. He collected and codified historical examples, and drew his own, including a font of Frutiger Symbols for Linotype and the playful Frutiger Stones. He cut abstract shapes in wood to accompany the first chapter of Genesis and the Song of Songs, and he sawed shapes in slate to make sculptures. His skill with symbols made him a particularly adept designer of logos and wordmarks. Those for the Swiss Post Office and the PostBus with its posthorn, and the 'm' for French Réunion des musées nationaux, are among the best known.

In 1988 Frutiger returned to the theme of sanserifs. In spite of his original aversion to Futura-like sanserifs that had led to the design of Univers, he undertook a design inspired by the constructivism of the 1930s, to be called Avenir. Successful typefaces in this category, such as ITC Avant Garde Gothic, were display faces; a geometric text type was a challenge that Frutiger relished. The subtle differences between Futura and Avenir are a case study in the value of a highly refined typographic sensibility.

The progression of sanserifs – Univers, Frutiger, Avenir – lacked one remaining design to complete the suite: an American Gothic in the idiom of Franklin Gothic, Trade Gothic and News Gothic. The result was Vectora, a sanserif characterized by a generous x-height, and equipped with small capitals and old-style figures.

In 1997, after Frutiger had left Paris to return to Switzerland and his native Bern, Linotype proposed to make a new version of Univers. The original Univers had become corrupted over 40 years through adaptations to different typesetting systems. The decision to return to the version of Deberny & Peignot delighted Frutiger, who took enthusiastic advantage of Linotype's initiative to add ultra-light and ultra-bold styles to the original family.

Another collaboration with Linotype was the "Type before Gutenberg" series suggested by Frutiger. The idea, to revisit pre-typographic alphabetic forms, gave Frutiger the opportunity to return to his thesis at the Kunstgewerbeschule in Zürich and make typefaces derived from the lettering he had so painstakingly cut in wood as a student. Herculanum, Capitalis (a Roman lapidary alphabet with accompanying symbols), Pompeijana, and Rusticana were Frutiger's contributions to this project. Nami, a design based on sketches done as a 24-year-old, was finally released with help from Akira Kobayashi at Linotype when Frutiger was 79.

It is possible to trace a number of influences on Frutiger as a designer. He felt an affinity between his father's work with woven textiles and his own with type on the printed page; he admired the black paper cutout decorations that were the folk art of

5

4 – Black and white. From Frutiger's
sketch book, 1949
5 – The Frutiger family at the opening
party of the studio Vache noir, Arcueil,
Paris, 1962
6 – Paper cutout from the Life cycle:
birth, ca. 1980

his birthplace in the Bernese Ober-
land; he owed much to the teaching of
Willimann and Käch in Zürich, to the
advice and friendship of Emil Ruder
in Basle, to the confidence in him
shown by Charles Peignot in Paris,
but in the end he stands *sui generis*.
What he learned from history or from
teaching he transmuted into something recognizable as uniquely his
own. The letters he made, their stems,
strokes, curves, counters, spaces, have
the integrity of a singular vision. Erich
Alb, a long-standing friend, said Frutiger was a designer with the equivalent
of a musician's perfect pitch, his hand
could not draw a bad line.

The passing of Adrian Frutiger and
of Hermann Zapf, within weeks of
each other, took from us the two giants
of a critical period of typographic
history: the transition from metal
foundry type, via the interregnum of
photocomposition, to the digital world
we now live in. It is extraordinary that
two designers, each as brilliant as any
in the history of type, had the training

and aptitude to lead the way through
a technical revolution with standards
of design that never wavered. They
designed different letters, but they had
the same goal: to put before the reader
typefaces, however they were made,
that were as beautiful as they were
functional.

Written for AGI Alliance Graphique
Internationale on 18 September 2015.
Images were kindly provided by
Mr. Erich Alb.

6

52

David Bowie
(1947–2016)
was facing his own
mortality with
Blackstar album

TEXT BY DAN HOWARTH

The cover of David Bowie's *Blackstar* album, released just days before his death, was designed to reflect the musician's mortality, according to his long-time graphic design collaborator Jonathan Barnbrook.

Blackstar, represented by a ★ symbol, was released on 8 January 2016 – Bowie's 69th birthday. The musician died two days later, and the album has since been interpreted as a poignant farewell and has topped charts worldwide.

The album artwork was one of five that Barnbrook worked on with Bowie in the last 15 years, making the British designer one of the recording star's closest and longest-serving collaborators.

In a recent interview with *Dezeen*, Barnbrook explained how he would work directly with Bowie rather than via his management team, discussing ideas via email or Skype.

"He always wanted to do something interesting, often to the annoyance of the record company," Barnbrook said. "He understood the value of the image

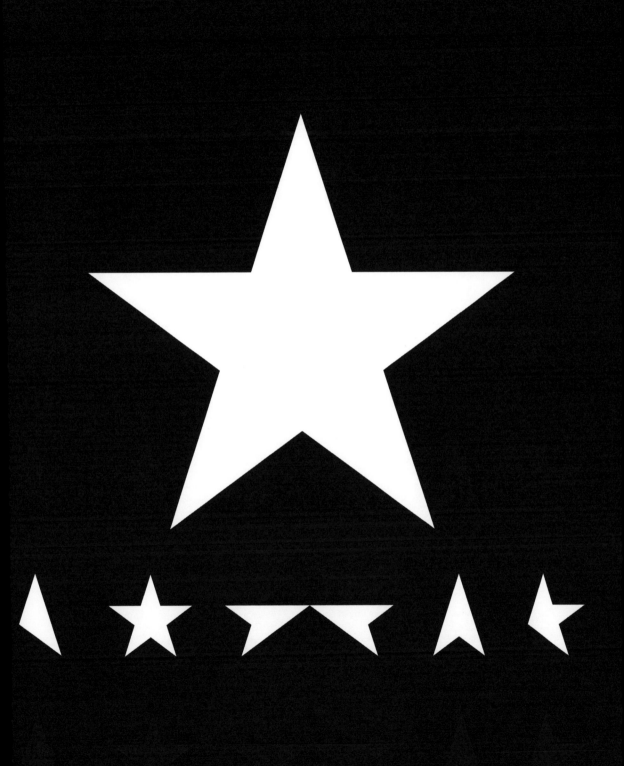

on a record cover, when other people had forgotten about it."

The designer added that Bowie was, more than anyone else, the artist responsible for bringing "art-school thinking into the mainstream".

Barnbrook's cover for Bowie's last record positions a large black star in the centre of a white background. The design is simple, but full of symbolism, he told *Dezeen*.

"This was a man who was facing his own mortality," said Barnbrook. "The Blackstar symbol [★], rather than writing 'Blackstar', has as a sort of finality, a darkness, a simplicity, which is a representation of the music."

"It's subsided a bit now, but a lot of people said it was a bullshit cover when it came out, that it took five minutes to design," he added. "But I think there is a misunderstanding about the simplicity."

The use of abstract shapes was developed from Barnbrook's previous controversial cover for *The Next Day* album. The design features a white square covering an old photo of Bowie and was influenced by Constructivist art.

The black star graphic also carries deeper meanings, said Barnbrook.

"The idea of mortality is in there, and of course the idea of a black hole sucking in everything, the Big Bang, the start of the universe, if there is an end of the universe," Barnbrook said. "These are things that relate to mortality."

For the vinyl edition, the star is cut out from the black sleeve so the record inside is visible.

"The fact that you can see the record as a physical thing that degrades, it gets scratched as soon as it comes into being, that is a comment on mortality too," said Barnbrook.

Graphic designer Jonathan Barnbrook (49) trained at London's Saint Martin's School of Art and Royal College of Art. He has designed a number of typefaces, many of which featured in a 2007 exhibition of his work titled *Friendly Fire*. He also worked on a book for British artist Damien Hirst, which ultimately led to his collaboration with Bowie.

The pair created five album covers together and each design proved divisive with both critics and fans.

"I hope they are a fitting tribute to his amazing creative life," said Barnbrook. "He's one of the people who most brought the avant-garde or intellectualism, or art-school thinking, into the mainstream."

This article was first published on www.dezeen.com and is reprinted with permission.

Contributors

Reza Abedini is a graphic designer and visual artist creating work that contains many historical and traditional references. He lives and works between Iran, Lebanon and the Netherlands.

Dr. Pedro Amado is an Assistant Professor in the Department of Communication and Arts at the University of Aveiro, dividing his efforts between brand design, digital interfaces and tinkering with type. He has organized conferences and workshops since 2007 and is a Portuguese country delegate for ATypI.

Phil Baines is a graphic designer and Professor of Typography at Central Saint Martins, London.

Dr. Andreu Balius is a type designer and runs TypeRepublic foundry based in Barcelona. He holds a PhD in Design from the University of Southampton.

Stephen Banham is a Melbourne-based typographer, writer and educator.

John D. Berry is an editor and typographer who writes and speaks about typography and design worldwide. He is the honorary president of ATypI and the director of the Scripta Typographic Institute.

Filip Blažek is a graphic designer, typographer and a teacher at the Academy of Arts, Architecture and Design in Prague. He regularly contributes to professional periodicals in the field of graphic design and is the Czech country delegate for ATypI.

Veronika Burian is a type designer and co-founder of the independent type foundry TypeTogether, publishing award-winning typefaces and collaborating on tailored typefaces for a variety of clients. She also continues to give lectures and workshops at international conferences and universities.

Matthew Carter is a type designer with 60 years' experience in typographic technologies, ranging from hand-cut punches to computer fonts. After a long association with the Linotype companies he was a co-founder of Bitstream Inc. in 1981, a digital type foundry where he worked for ten years. Carter is now a principal of Carter & Cone Type Inc., designers and producers of original typefaces, in Cambridge, Massachusetts.

Christopher Çolak is a communication and type designer currently working as an art director in Istanbul. He is also the Turkish country delegate for ATypI.

Dr. Jo De Baerdemaeker is a Belgian typeface designer and researcher. He holds an MA in Typeface Design and PhD from the University of Reading and teaches at LUCA School of Arts (Brussels), the Plantin Institute of Typography (Antwerp), and the European Lettering Institute (Bruges). In 2012 he founded Studio Type in Antwerp. He is a member of the ATypI Board of Directors.

Catherine Dixon is a designer, writer and Senior Lecturer in Typography at Central Saint Martins, London.

Tobias Frere-Jones is a US type designer based in New York City. He has designed over seven hundred typefaces. He teaches typeface design at the Yale School of Art MFA programme.

Dr. Shelley Gruendler, founder of Type Camp, is a typographer, designer and educator. She holds a PhD and MA in History and Theory of Typography and Graphic Communication from the University of Reading and a Bachelor of Environmental Design in Graphic Design from North Carolina State University.

Dan Howarth is a British architecture, design and fashion journalist based in New York, currently working as US editor for Dezeen.

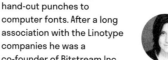

Feike de Jong is an award-winning journalist and urban researcher in Mexico City.

Eva Kašáková is a graphic designer living in Slovakia. She is a co-founder of the SELF festival.

Rob Keller is a typeface designer who runs the type foundry motaitalic.com and blogs at youshouldliketypetoo.com.

Jan Kubasiewicz is a Professor of design and the founder and coordinator (2000–2015) of Dynamic Media Institute, a graduate design programme at the Massachusetts College of Art and Design in Boston.

Linda Kudrnovská is a natural born critic and writer. She has been the editor-in-chief of *Typo* magazine for the past decade and regularly contributes to a number of other periodicals. She is a member of the ATypI Board of Directors.

Indra Kupferschmid is a German typographer, consultant and Professor at HBKsaar.

Jean-Baptiste Levée is a typeface designer and educator and runs Production Type foundry.

Dionysis Livanis is a London-based graphic designer and visual artist. He holds an MA in Typo/Graphic Studies, has worked in branding and design agencies in Greece, Spain and the UK, and has contributed to international design publications.

Mathieu Lommen has written several monographs on book and type design and lettering; he is a curator at the University of Amsterdam.

Martin Majoor is a Dutch type and book designer who works between the Netherlands and Poland. He designed Scala, Telefont, Seria, Nexus and Questa. Majoor has taught typography at several schools of fine art and given numerous lectures throughout the world. He has written articles for various magazines and contributed to several books on typography.

Fernanda Martins is a graphic designer, typographer and researcher in love with the Amazon region.

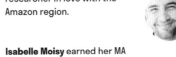

Isabelle Moisy earned her MA in Visual Anthropology from the University of Lyon II and completed a research programme at EnsadLab in Paris. In 2009 she joined *étapes:* magazine and was co-editor-in-chief between 2012 and 2017.

Darío Manuel Muhafara is a type designer, the coordinator of the Master's course in Typography at Buenos Aires University and ATypI delegate from Argentina.

María Laura Nieto is a designer, Professor and researcher at Buenos Aires University.

Martin Pecina is a Czech type designer primarily focused on book design. In 2011 he published *Knihy a typografie*, a book about books and typography.

Yves Peters is a graphic designer, rock drummer and father of three who tries to be critical about typography without coming across as a snob. The former editor-in-chief of *The FontFeed*, he has found a new home at FontShop News. His ability to identify most typefaces on sight is utterly useless in daily life.

César Puertas is a graphic and type designer, founder of Typograma type foundry and an Associate Professor at the Universidad Nacional de Colombia. He holds a Master's degree in Type and Media from KABK in The Hague and is the Colombian country delegate for ATypI.

Vítor Quelhas is an Adjunct Professor of Communication Design in the Department of Image Arts at Porto Polytechnic Institute's School of Music and Performing Arts. He is finishing his PhD in Design at the University of Aveiro. The Type Directors Club has officially recognized his work with two Certificates of Typographic Excellence. He is a Portuguese country delegate for ATypI.

Dan Reynolds lives in Berlin with his wife, son and dog. He draws type and writes about other designers – mostly dead ones.

Silvia Sfligiotti is a graphic designer, educator and design critic. She is the co-founder of Alizarina studio and teaches at ISIA Urbino and Scuola Politecnica di Design Milano. In 2010 she co-edited the book *Open Projects* and exhibition of the same name at the 21st International Poster and Graphic Design Festival in Chaumont. Since 2012 she has been co-editor of the Italian graphic design magazine *Progetto grafico*.

Jakub Skalický is a film director, screenwriter and music director. His work primarily focuses on alternative culture and journalism. For the past five years he has been interested in food and energy independence, which he is actively pursuing on his family farm in eastern Bohemia.

Teal Triggs is Professor of Graphic Design and Associate Dean, Royal College of Art, London.

Liron Lavi Turkenich is a typeface designer and researcher. She holds a Master's degree in Typeface Design from the University of Reading and a degree in Visual Communications. She finds great interest in multilingual typeface design, and specializes in Hebrew and Amharic.

Carol Wahler has been Executive Director with the Type Directors Club since 1983. She has been editor of the TDC newsletter *Letterspace* and integrally involved in other committees (such as the annual competition, annual book *Typography*, and the traveling exhibits). She has lectured about the history of the TDC to universities and schools around the globe.

Onur Yazıcıgil is a typographer and educator who currently lives and works in Istanbul, Turkey.

Name index